WOOD PELLET
GRILL SMOKER
COOKBOOK

JOSHUA SMITH

TABLE OF CONTENTS

CONVERSION CHART

Liquid Measure

8 ounces =	1 cup
2 cups =	1 pint
16 ounces =	1 pint
4 cups =	1 quart
1 gill =	1/2 cup or 1/4 pint
2 pints =	1 quart
4 quarts =	1 gallon
31.5 gal. =	1 barrel
3 tsp =	1 tbsp
2 tbsp =	1/8 cup or 1 fluid ounce
4 tbsp =	1/4 cup
8 tbsp =	1/2 cup
1 pinch =	1/8 tsp or less
1 tsp =	60 drops

Conversion of US Liquid Measure to Metric System

1 fluid oz. =	29.573 milliliters
1 cup =	230 milliliters
1 quart =	.94635 liters
1 gallon =	3.7854 liters
.033814 fluid ounce =	1 milliliter
3.3814 fluid ounces =	1 deciliter
33.814 fluid oz. or 1.0567 qt.=	1 liter

Dry Measure

2 pints =	1 quart
4 quarts =	1 gallon
8 quarts =	2 gallons or 1 peck
4 pecks =	8 gallons or 1 bushel
16 ounces =	1 pound
2000 lbs. =	1 ton

Conversion of US Weight and Mass Measure to Metric System

.0353 ounces =	1 gram
1/4 ounce =	7 grams
1 ounce =	28.35 grams
4 ounces =	113.4 grams
8 ounces =	226.8 grams
1 pound =	454 grams
2.2046 pounds =	1 kilogram
.98421 long ton or 1.1023 short tons =	1 metric ton

Linear Measure

12 inches =	1 foot
3 feet =	1 yard
5.5 yards =	1 rod
40 rods =	1 furlong
8 furlongs (5280 feet) =	1 mile
6080 feet =	1 nautical mile

Conversion of US Linear Measure to Metric System

1 inch =	2.54 centimeters
1 foot =	.3048 meters
1 yard =	.9144 meters
1 mile =	1609.3 meters or 1.6093 kilometers
.03937 in. =	1 millimeter
.3937 in.=	1 centimeter
3.937 in.=	1 decimeter
39.37 in.=	1 meter
3280.8 ft. or .62137 miles =	1 kilometer

To convert a Fahrenheit temperature to Centigrade, do the following:
a. Subtract 32   b. Multiply by 5   c. Divide by 9

To convert Centigrade to Fahrenheit, do the following:
a. Multiply by 9   b. Divide by 5   c. Add 32

Introduction

Pellet Smokers and Grills are currently among the most popular items in the market. While a few people attribute this popularity to increased usage and effective marketing, the majority agree that their unmatched popularity stems from the product's effectiveness.

In contrast to traditional grills, Pellet Smokers and Grills stand out as exceptionally versatile, automated, and user-friendly. They offer a revolutionary grilling experience, ensuring the desired flavor every time. These grills are not only the ideal choice but also the best solution for cooking any type of meat healthily. They offer a range of cooking methods, from smoking ingredients to slow roasting, baking pizzas, and perfectly grilling steaks.

Despite their growing popularity, many people are still unfamiliar with this innovative appliance. So, what exactly is a Wood Pellet Smoker and Grill, and how does one use it?

1. What is a pellet smoker and grill?

To provide a clear explanation of the Wood Pellet Smoker and Grill, let's begin by defining this grilling appliance. Pellet Smokers and Grills are essentially electric outdoor smokers and grills that exclusively use wood pellets as fuel. These pellets, known for their capsule size, are highly regarded for their ability to impart enhanced flavors and tastes to smoked meats.

What sets wood pellets apart as a fuel source is their versatility. They can be used for grilling, smoking, roasting, braising, and even baking, all guided by straightforward instructions. Additionally, Pellet Smokers and Grills are equipped with a control board that enables automatic maintenance of your desired temperature for extended periods.

2. Why choose to use a wood pellet Smoker and Grill?

The uniqueness of Pellet Smokers and Grills lies in their exceptional blend of flavor and versatility. Indeed, these grills create a remarkable fusion of sublime tastes and incredible deliciousness. They are outstanding appliances for those who enjoy the taste of charcoal grilling but don't want to forgo the traditional flavors achieved with ovens.

What's more, Pellet Smokers and Grills offer convenience through simplicity. With just the press of a button, you can grill, roast, bake, braise, and smoke your favorite meats. The experience is further enhanced by their automatic nature; you can set the temperature, walk away, and return

to enjoy the delectable flavors you've been craving. But how exactly do we use a Pellet Smoker and Grill?

Pellet Smokers and Grills operate using advanced digital technology and various mechanical components. These grills are ignited, and their temperature is typically set using a digital control board. They function by employing an algorithm to calculate the precise number of pellets required to maintain the perfect temperature. Each Wood Pellet Grill comes equipped with a rotating auger that automatically feeds the fire from the hopper, ensuring a consistent temperature. As the food cooks, the grill continues to add the exact amount of pellets needed to sustain the ideal cooking temperature. But what can you cook with a Pellet Smoker and Grill?

Thanks to their versatile capabilities for smoking, grilling, braising, and functioning as a kitchen oven, Wood Pellet Smokers and Grills can be used to prepare an endless array of dishes and recipes. There is virtually no limit to what you can cook, including hot dogs, chicken, vegetables, seafood, rabbit, brisket, turkey, and much more. The cooking process is straightforward: simply load your favorite wood pellets into the hopper, set the desired temperature on the controller, and place the food on the grill. The pellets will maintain the temperature and keep burning efficiently.

Pellet Smokers and Grills are electric and typically require a standard 110v outlet to power the digital board, fan, and auger.

There is a broad range of Pellet Smoker and Grill types, including electric pellet smokers, wood-fired grills, wood pellet grills, and wood pellet smokers. Numerous brands offer Wood Pellet Smokers and Grills, with Traeger being one of the most renowned.

For example, Traeger is recognized as one of the world's leading brands of pellet grills. Joe Traeger, the inventor of the pellet grill in the mid-1980s, gave his name to this invention. After the expiration of the Traeger patent, a variety of other Pellet Smokers and Grills emerged on the market.

Roasting and grilling are two methods pivotal in infusing meat with flavorful tastes. Grilling not only offers a healthier cooking technique but also helps retain nutrients in the meat. The Wood Pellet Smoker and Grill is an outstanding replacement for traditional grilling methods like barbecuing, offering numerous benefits. Here are some of the most well-known advantages of using a Pellet Smoker and Grill:

Wood Pellet Smokers and Grills are specifically designed to enhance flavors and aromas by using wood pellets as fuel. This method allows us to enjoy our favorite flavors with minimal ingredients and hardwood pellets.

9. Walnut: A strong-flavored wood, often mixed with lighter woods like pecan or apple due to its slight bitterness.

Best for smoking: Red meat and game birds.

10. Grape: Imparts a sweet berry flavor, best used with applewood chips.

Best for smoking: Poultry.

11. Mulberry: Similar to applewood, adds natural sweetness and a berry finish.

Best for smoking: Ham and chicken.

12. Mesquite: Known for its earthy, slightly harsh, and bitter flavor. Burns fast and hot, so it's not suitable for long grilling.

Best for smoking: Red meat and dark meat.

The Difference between Barbecuing and Smoking a Meat

There are two main methods of cooking meat that have gained popularity: smoking and barbecuing. Each method is distinct and requires specific cooking equipment, temperature control, and timing. Here's a detailed comparison between smoking and barbecuing:

BARBECUING MEAT

Barbecuing involves slow cooking the meat indirectly over low heat, typically between 200 to 250 degrees Fahrenheit. This method is ideal for tough meats like beef brisket, whole pigs, turkeys, or pork shoulders, which require slow cooking over low heat to become moist and tender. The result is extremely tender and flavorful meat, often characterized by meat falling off the bones. During barbecuing, it's important to frequently refill the fuel but do so quickly to prevent the meat from drying out, as lifting the lid of the burner exposes it to air.

For barbecuing, preheat the grill until it's hot. Light enough charcoal or briquettes so that their fire is suitable for cooking. Season the meat in the meantime, and once the grill reaches the perfect cooking temperature, place the seasoned meat on it. Maintaining the right grill temperature is crucial to prevent the meat from sticking to the grate.

Equipment: A fire pit, grill, or a charcoal burner with a lid. Fuel: Lump wood charcoal, charcoal briquettes, or a combination of wood chips such as apple, cherry, and oak. Best for smoking: Large cuts of meat like brisket, whole chicken, sausages, jerky, pork, and ribs. Temperature: 190 to 300 degrees Fahrenheit. Timing: Ranges from 2 hours to a whole day.

SMOKING MEAT

Smoking is one of the oldest cooking techniques, dating back to the earliest people living in caves. Originally a method for preserving food, its popularity has endured over time. Smoking is closely related to barbecuing and is renowned as the best method to bring out the rich and deep flavors in meat, creating heavenly tastes especially when the meat is smoked until it falls off the bone.

During smoking, food is cooked at temperatures below 200 degrees Fahrenheit. This method requires a considerable amount of time and patience, as it infuses a woody flavor into the meat, making it silky and tender enough to fall off the bone. There are three primary methods of smoking: cold smoke, hot smoke, and adding liquid smoke. Among these, liquid smoke is becoming increasingly popular due to its ability to control the smoky flavor and its immediate effect on the meat.

Another method is water smoking, which uses a water smoker specially designed to incorporate water into the smoking process. The water aids in temperature control, making it ideal for large cuts of meat that need to be smoked for extended periods.

Equipment: A closed container or a high-tech smoker. Fueling: The container requires an external smoke source. Wood chips are burned to impart a smoky flavor to the meat. However, frequent checks are necessary to monitor and adjust the smoking temperature. Best for smoking: Large cuts of meat like brisket, whole chicken, pork, and ribs. Temperature: 68 to 176 degrees Fahrenheit. Timing: Ranges from 1 hour to 2 weeks.

Chapter 2:
Tools, Maintenance and Cleaning Procedures

Before you dive into the world of grilling and barbecuing, it's essential to have the right tools to make the process smoother. Here are a few must-haves:

A Pair of Scissors and A Set of Knives: These are absolutely indispensable. Keep them within easy reach, or consider purchasing a new set if your current one isn't up to par. You'll frequently need knives for cutting a lot of meat, both raw and cooked. Scissors also come in handy for trimming choice cuts of meat and other preparatory tasks. A highly recommended knife is the 14-inch slicing knife, especially one with a hollow edge, which is ideal for slicing large portions of poultry, roasts, and briskets.

A Digital Meat Thermometer: This tool is crucial. Temperature plays a significant role when working with meats, and it's not just about the surface temperature. Monitoring the internal temperature is key. Even if you have a wood pellet smoker grill with multiple probes, having an additional digital meat thermometer is wise. It helps you double-check that everything is cooking perfectly.

A Smoker Box: A smoker box is a versatile tool that allows you to cold smoke a variety of items, including jerky, salmon, nuts, meats, and even cheese. It's also useful for storing and keeping your food warm or at the proper serving temperature. Consider contacting the manufacturer to see if they can equip your unit with a smoker box. It's a worthwhile addition that you'll appreciate having!

Searing Grates: There is a wide range of searing grates available, and the right choice depends on the make and model of your wood pellet smoker grill. The beauty of searing grates is their ability to accommodate both direct and indirect

flame techniques. Reach out to your manufacturer to determine the best type of searing grates for your grill. With a searing grate, you can grill various cuts of meat to achieve high-quality results, the kind that was once exclusive to upscale steakhouses.

Open Flame Tech, Flame Zone, and Direct Flame: If you have a high-quality wood pellet smoker grill, it likely features technology that allows for grilling and barbecuing with a direct flame. In the past, cooking was primarily done with indirect flames, but with modern advancements, you can now grill using direct flame technology (though different manufacturers might have different names for it; essentially, it's the same concept). The best models even allow grilling at temperatures exceeding 500 degrees Fahrenheit.

A Rib Rack: This accessory enables you to cook anywhere from four to eight slabs of spare ribs at once. The number of ribs you can cook simultaneously depends on the surface area of your wood pellet smoker grill.

A Chicken Wing/Leg Hanger: If you're looking to cook chicken wings or legs, these hangers are essential. They are affordable and widely available – a quick Google search should reveal where to purchase them. These hangers facilitate smoke penetration into the meat and ensure even heat distribution across the grill, resulting in perfectly cooked chicken. As an added benefit, they allow fat to drip off the chicken, making it a healthier option. They make basting a breeze!

Barbecue Insulated Gloves: I appreciate these gloves for their flexibility and lightweight design, yet they provide all the protection needed when handling hot food. To maintain them, simply wash by hand using mild soap. Rinse the gloves, hang them up, and let them drip dry.

Teflon Coated Fiberglass Mats: These mats are ideal for indirect cooking, effectively preventing food from sticking to your grill grates. They are FDA-approved and dishwasher-safe, adding to their convenience.

A Meat Slicer: For efficient meat slicing, opt for a seven-inch slicer. It will save you the hassle of slicing food by hand. Remember, it's 2019 – the caveman era is long gone. Modernizing your kitchen with one of these slicers is a smart move.

A Nonstick Grilling Tray: This is incredibly useful for cooking fish, vegetables, or any small, crumbly foods. The tray is easy to clean with soap and water, making it quickly ready for its next use.

A Pigtail Food Flipper: Despite its name, this tool does not involve actual pig tails. It features a nicely tapered shaft with a sharp, spiral snare at the end. It's used to flip food by simply piercing the edge of the item and flipping it over. It's versatile for most foods, though perhaps not the best choice for fish and vegetables.

A Griddle: If you're aiming to create a breakfast feast, then a griddle is a must-have! It's perfect for cooking a variety of breakfast favorites such as eggs, French toast, hash browns, bacon, pancakes, and sausages.

A Liquid Flavor Injector: For incredibly juicy meats, a liquid flavor injector is essential. It allows you to infuse your meats with brines, herbs, spices, and marinades, resulting in flavors so rich they'll make your taste buds rejoice.

A Bluetooth Remote Control: This isn't for playing music from your phone on your grill — that's just a joke. With a Bluetooth remote con-

trol, you can monitor and adjust the settings of your wood pellet smoker grill remotely. It's incredibly convenient, as it saves you from constantly moving in and out of the house to check on your meats.

A Grill Cover: Protect your wood pellet smoker grill from weather damage and natural wear and tear with a grill cover. It keeps your smoker grill dry and in good condition when not in use.

Storing Your Wood Pellets

The best way to store wood pellets is in a dry place, such as a shed or garage. If you have a wooden pallet, it's ideal for keeping your pellets off the ground. The reason for a dry storage area is to prevent the pellets from getting wet or de-

grading due to atmospheric moisture, especially over time. Once affected by moisture, pellets may not light properly and could potentially damage your auger.

To prevent this, as soon as you open a bag of wood pellets, store the remaining pellets in a charcoal or wood pellet dispenser. They can also be stored in new trash cans, plastic buckets with lids, large pet food containers, or any airtight container. Ensure these containers are kept in a dry area like a shed or garage.

Cleaning Your Wood Pellet Smoker Grill

If you tend to neglect cleaning appliances like toasters, ovens, or grills, it's crucial to change that habit with your wood pellet smoker grill. Keeping it clean is vital and only requires a few minutes after each use.

Why is cleanliness important? A clean grill ensures that the smoke flavoring your meals is fresh, not stale. Using foil on your grease drip pan is recommended, and it should be replaced after two to four cooking sessions, or after each lengthy session. If you opt not to use foil, be diligent in removing any residue that builds up on the drip pan to avoid burning old, rancid grease, which can create unpleasant fumes and affect your meals.

The best practice is to clean the grill immediately after each cooking session. Clean the hot grates with a wire brush specifically designed for barbecues and thoroughly wipe both sides of the grates with paper towels. Never skimp on this step. Wear rubber gloves, preferably disposable, for protection while cleaning.

CHAPTER 3
PORK RECIPES

APPLEWOOD SMOKED PULLED PORK

Preparation Time: 30 minutes (plus overnight marinating)

Cooking Time: 6 hours

Servings: 4-6

Ingredients:

- 2 racks of pork ribs (about 6 pounds)
- 1/4 cup brown sugar
- 2 tablespoons paprika
- 1 tablespoon garlic powder
- 1 tablespoon onion powder
- 1 tablespoon ground black pepper
- 1 tablespoon kosher salt
- 2 teaspoons cayenne pepper (optional, for heat)
- 2 cups apple cider vinegar (for spraying)
- Hickory wood pellets for the smoker

Directions:

1. **Prep the Ribs:** Remove the membrane from the back of the ribs. In a bowl, mix brown sugar, paprika, garlic powder, onion powder, black pepper, kosher salt, and cayenne pepper. Rub this mixture evenly over the ribs. Let the ribs marinate in the refrigerator overnight.

2. **Preheat the Smoker:** Preheat your wood pellet smoker grill to 225°F (107°C) using hickory wood pellets.

3. **Smoke the Ribs:** Place the ribs in the smoker. Smoke for about 3 hours. Every hour, spray the ribs with apple cider vinegar to keep them moist.

4. **Wrap the Ribs:** After 3 hours, wrap the ribs in aluminum foil and return them to the smoker. Cook for another 2 hours.

5. **Finish and Serve:** Unwrap the ribs and place them back in the smoker for an additional hour, or until they reach an internal temperature of 195°F (90°C). Let them rest for 10 minutes before serving.

Macronutrients (per serving, approximate):

Calories: 600 kcal - **Carbohydrates:** 12g - **Protein:** 44g - **Fat:** 42g

CHERRY WOOD SMOKED PORK SHOULDER

Preparation Time: 20 minutes (plus overnight marinating)

Cooking Time: 10 hours

Servings: 8-10

Ingredients:

- 1 pork shoulder (about 8 pounds)
- 1/4 cup apple cider vinegar
- 1/4 cup Worcestershire sauce
- 1/4 cup brown sugar
- 2 tablespoons smoked paprika
- 1 tablespoon garlic powder
- 1 tablespoon onion powder
- 1 tablespoon ground black pepper
- 1 tablespoon kosher salt
- 2 teaspoons dry mustard
- Applewood pellets for the smoker

Directions:

1. **Marinate the Pork**: In a bowl, mix apple cider vinegar, Worcestershire sauce, brown sugar, smoked paprika, garlic powder, onion powder, black pepper, kosher salt, and dry mustard. Rub this mixture over the pork shoulder and let it marinate in the refrigerator overnight.

2. **Preheat the Smoker**: Preheat your wood pellet smoker grill to 225°F (107°C) using applewood pellets.

3. **Smoke the Pork**: Place the pork shoulder in the smoker. Smoke for about 6 hours.

4. **Wrap and Continue Smoking**: Wrap the pork shoulder in aluminum foil and continue smoking for another 4 hours, or until the internal temperature reaches 195°F (90°C).

5. **Rest and Serve**: Remove the pork from the smoker and let it rest for 30 minutes. Shred the pork using two forks and serve.

Macronutrients (per serving, approximate):

Calories: 530 kcal - **Carbohydrates:** 6g - **Protein:** 75g - **Fat:** 22g

SMOKED PORK BELLY BURNT ENDS

Preparation Time: 15 minutes

Cooking Time: 6 hours

Servings: 6-8

Ingredients:

- 3 pounds pork belly, skinless
- 1/4 cup honey
- 1/4 cup brown sugar
- 2 tablespoons apple cider vinegar
- 2 tablespoons barbecue rub (your choice)
- 1 tablespoon paprika
- 1 teaspoon garlic powder
- 1 teaspoon onion powder
- Salt and pepper to taste
- Your choice of wood pellets for smoking (hickory or applewood work well)

Directions:

1. **Prepare the Pork Belly**: Cut the pork belly into 1.5-inch cubes. In a bowl, mix together barbecue rub, paprika, garlic powder, onion powder, salt, and pepper. Coat the pork belly cubes evenly with this mixture.

2. **Preheat the Smoker**: Preheat your wood pellet smoker grill to 250°F (121°C) using your choice of wood pellets.

3. **Smoke the Pork Belly**: Place the seasoned pork belly cubes on the smoker grate. Smoke for about 3 hours, or until the outsides are crispy and caramelized.

4. **Glaze the Pork Belly**: In a separate bowl, mix honey, brown sugar, and apple cider vinegar. Remove the pork belly cubes from the smoker, toss them in the glaze, then return them to the smoker. Smoke for an additional 1-2 hours.

5. **Finish and Serve**: The pork belly burnt ends are done when they have a deep caramelized exterior and are tender inside. Remove from the smoker and let rest for a few minutes before serving.

Macronutrients (per serving, approximate):

Calories: 650 kcal - **Carbohydrates**: 15g - **Protein**: 14g - **Fat**: 60g

MAPLE-GLAZED SMOKED PORK CHOPS

Preparation Time: 20 minutes

Cooking Time: 1.5 hours

Servings: 4

Ingredients:

- 4 pork chops, bone-in (about 8 oz each)
- 1/4 cup maple syrup
- 2 tablespoons apple cider vinegar
- 1 tablespoon Dijon mustard
- 1 teaspoon smoked paprika
- 1 teaspoon garlic powder
- Salt and pepper to taste
- Your choice of wood pellets for smoking (applewood or cherry work well)

Directions:

1. **Prepare the Pork Chops**: Season the pork chops on both sides with smoked paprika, garlic powder, salt, and pepper.

2. **Create the Glaze**: In a small bowl, whisk together maple syrup, apple cider vinegar, and Dijon mustard. Set aside for glazing.

3. **Preheat the Smoker**: Preheat your wood pellet smoker grill to 250°F (121°C) using your choice of wood pellets.

4. **Smoke the Pork Chops**: Place the seasoned pork chops on the smoker grate. Smoke for about 1 hour.

5. **Glaze and Finish**: Brush the pork chops with the maple glaze and continue smoking for an additional 30 minutes, or until the internal temperature reaches 145°F (63°C).

Macronutrients (per serving, approximate):

Calories: 350 kcal - **Carbohydrates**: 15g - **Protein**: 35g - **Fat**: 16g

MESQUITE SMOKED PORK LOIN

Preparation Time: 15 minutes

Cooking Time: 3 hours

Servings: 6

Ingredients:

- 1 pork loin (about 3 pounds)
- 1/4 cup olive oil
- 3 tablespoons brown sugar
- 2 tablespoons paprika
- 1 tablespoon garlic powder
- 1 tablespoon onion powder
- 1 teaspoon dried thyme
- Salt and pepper to taste
- Mesquite wood pellets for smoking

Directions:

1. **Prepare the Pork Loin**: Rub the pork loin with olive oil. In a small bowl, mix together brown sugar, paprika, garlic powder, onion powder, thyme, salt, and pepper. Apply this rub evenly over the pork loin.

2. **Preheat the Smoker**: Preheat your wood pellet smoker grill to 250°F (121°C) using mesquite wood pellets.

3. **Smoke the Pork Loin**: Place the seasoned pork loin on the smoker grate. Smoke for about 2.5 hours, or until the internal temperature reaches 145°F (63°C).

4. **Rest and Serve**: Remove the pork loin from the smoker and let it rest for 10-15 minutes. This allows the juices to redistribute throughout the meat.

5. **Slice and Enjoy**: Slice the pork loin and serve.

Macronutrients (per serving, approximate):

Calories: 310 kcal - **Carbohydrates:** 6g - **Protein:** 50g - **Fat:** 10g

PECAN WOOD SMOKED HAM

Preparation Time: 30 minutes (plus overnight resting)

Cooking Time: 4 hours

Servings: 8-10

Ingredients:

- 1 fully cooked bone-in ham (about 8-10 pounds)
- 1 cup brown sugar
- 1/4 cup honey
- 1/4 cup Dijon mustard
- 2 tablespoons apple cider vinegar
- 1 teaspoon ground cinnamon
- 1 teaspoon ground cloves
- Pecan wood pellets for smoking

Directions:

1. **Prepare the Glaze**: In a bowl, mix brown sugar, honey, Dijon mustard, apple cider vinegar, cinnamon, and cloves to make the glaze.

2. **Score the Ham**: Score the surface of the ham in a diamond pattern. Apply half of the glaze evenly over the ham. Let the ham rest in the refrigerator overnight.

3. **Preheat the Smoker**: Preheat your wood pellet smoker grill to 225°F (107°C) using pecan wood pellets.

4. **Smoke the Ham**: Place the ham in the smoker. Smoke for about 3 hours. Halfway through, apply the remaining glaze.

5. **Finish and Serve**: Continue smoking until the internal temperature of the ham reaches 140°F (60°C). Remove the ham from the smoker and let it rest for 15-20 minutes before slicing.

Macronutrients (per serving, approximate):

Calories: 450 kcal - **Carbohydrates**: 20g - **Protein**: 50g - **Fat**: 20g

BACON-WRAPPED PORK TENDERLOIN

Preparation Time: 20 minutes

Cooking Time: 2.5 hours

Servings: 4-6

Ingredients:

- 2 pork tenderloins (about 1 pound each)
- 1 pound bacon
- 2 tablespoons brown sugar
- 1 tablespoon paprika
- 1 teaspoon garlic powder
- 1 teaspoon onion powder
- Salt and pepper to taste
- Your choice of wood pellets for smoking (hickory or applewood work well)

Directions:

1. **Prepare the Pork Tenderloins**: In a small bowl, mix brown sugar, paprika, garlic powder, onion powder, salt, and pepper. Rub this mixture all over the pork tenderloins.

2. **Wrap with Bacon**: Wrap each pork tenderloin with bacon slices, ensuring the entire surface is covered.

3. **Preheat the Smoker**: Preheat your wood pellet smoker grill to 225°F (107°C) using your choice of wood pellets.

4. **Smoke the Pork Tenderloins**: Place the bacon-wrapped pork tenderloins on the smoker grate. Smoke for about 2.5 hours, or until the internal temperature reaches 145°F (63°C).

5. **Rest and Serve**: Remove the pork tenderloins from the smoker and let them rest for 10 minutes. Slice and serve.

Macronutrients (per serving, approximate):

Calories: 520 kcal - **Carbohydrates:** 5g - **Protein:** 48g - **Fat:** 34g

SMOKED SAUSAGE LINKS WITH APPLE AND HICKORY

Preparation Time: 10 minutes

Cooking Time: 1.5 hours

Servings: 6

Ingredients:

- 2 pounds of your favorite sausage links (e.g., kielbasa, andouille)
- 1/2 cup apple juice
- 1 tablespoon olive oil
- 1 teaspoon garlic powder
- 1 teaspoon onion powder
- 1 teaspoon smoked paprika
- Salt and pepper to taste
- Apple and hickory wood pellets for smoking

Directions:

1. **Prepare the Sausage Links**: If not pre-seasoned, rub the sausage links with a mixture of olive oil, garlic powder, onion powder, smoked paprika, salt, and pepper.

2. **Preheat the Smoker**: Preheat your wood pellet smoker grill to 225°F (107°C), using a mix of apple and hickory wood pellets for a balanced, smoky flavor.

3. **Smoke the Sausage Links**: Place the sausage links on the smoker grate. Smoke for about 1.5 hours. If you have a smoker box or tray, add apple juice for added moisture and flavor.

4. **Check for Doneness**: The sausages are done when they reach an internal temperature of 160°F (71°C).

5. **Serve**: Remove the sausages from the smoker and let them rest for a few minutes. Slice and serve.

Macronutrients (per serving, approximate):

Calories: 330 kcal - **Carbohydrates**: 2g - **Protein**: 20g - **Fat**: 27g

SMOKED PORK BUTT

Preparation Time: 30 minutes (plus overnight marinating)

Cooking Time: 8 hours

Servings: 8-10

Ingredients:

- 1 pork butt (about 8 pounds)
- 1/2 cup bourbon
- 1/4 cup brown sugar
- 1/4 cup paprika
- 2 tablespoons salt
- 2 tablespoons garlic powder
- 2 tablespoons onion powder
- 1 tablespoon ground black pepper
- 1 tablespoon ground cumin
- 2 teaspoons cayenne pepper (optional for heat)
- Your choice of wood pellets for smoking (hickory or applewood work well)

Directions:

1. **Marinate the Pork**: In a bowl, combine bourbon, brown sugar, paprika, salt, garlic powder, onion powder, black pepper, cumin, and cayenne pepper. Rub this mixture all over the pork butt. Let the pork marinate in the refrigerator overnight.

2. **Preheat the Smoker**: Preheat your wood pellet smoker grill to 225°F (107°C) using your choice of wood pellets.

3. **Smoke the Pork Butt**: Place the marinated pork butt on the smoker grate. Smoke for about 8 hours, or until the internal temperature reaches 195°F (90°C).

4. **Rest and Serve**: Remove the pork butt from the smoker and let it rest for 30 minutes. Shred the pork using two forks and serve.

Macronutrients (per serving, approximate):

Calories: 520 kcal - **Carbohydrates**: 6g - **Protein**: 65g - **Fat**: 25g

SPICY SMOKED PORK SPARERIBS

Preparation Time: 20 minutes (plus overnight marinating)

Cooking Time: 6 hours

Servings: 4-6

Ingredients:

- 2 racks of pork spareribs (about 6 pounds)
- 1/4 cup apple cider vinegar
- 2 tablespoons olive oil
- 1/4 cup brown sugar
- 2 tablespoons chili powder
- 2 tablespoons paprika
- 1 tablespoon garlic powder
- 1 tablespoon onion powder
- 1 teaspoon cayenne pepper (adjust for heat preference)
- 1 teaspoon black pepper
- 1 teaspoon salt
- Your choice of wood pellets for smoking (hickory or mesquite work well)

Directions:

1. **Prepare the Ribs**: Remove the membrane from the back of the ribs. In a bowl, mix together apple cider vinegar and olive oil. In another bowl, combine brown sugar, chili powder, paprika, garlic powder, onion powder, cayenne pepper, black pepper, and salt. Brush the vinegar and oil mixture over the ribs, then rub the dry spice mix evenly onto them. Let the ribs marinate in the refrigerator overnight.

2. **Preheat the Smoker**: Preheat your wood pellet smoker grill to 225°F (107°C) using your choice of wood pellets.

3. **Smoke the Ribs**: Place the ribs in the smoker. Smoke for about 3 hours, spraying them occasionally with apple cider vinegar to keep them moist.

4. **Wrap the Ribs**: Wrap the ribs in aluminum foil and return them to the smoker. Cook for another 2 hours.

5. **Finish and Serve**: Unwrap the ribs and place them back in the smoker for an additional hour, or until they reach an internal temperature of 195°F (90°C). Let them rest for 10 minutes before serving.

Macronutrients (per serving, approximate):

Calories: 600 kcal - **Carbohydrates:** 12g - **Protein:** 44g - **Fat:** 42g

SMOKED BABY BACK RIBS WITH HONEY GLAZE

Preparation Time: 20 minutes (plus overnight marinating)

Cooking Time: 5 hours

Servings: 4-6

Ingredients:

- 2 racks of baby back ribs (about 4-5 pounds)
- 1/4 cup honey
- 2 tablespoons soy sauce
- 1/4 cup brown sugar
- 2 tablespoons paprika
- 1 tablespoon garlic powder
- 1 tablespoon onion powder
- 1 teaspoon ground black pepper
- 1 teaspoon salt
- Your choice of wood pellets for smoking (applewood or cherry work well)

Directions:

1. **Prepare the Ribs**: Remove the membrane from the back of the ribs. In a bowl, combine brown sugar, paprika, garlic powder, onion powder, black pepper, and salt. Rub this mixture evenly over the ribs. Let the ribs marinate in the refrigerator overnight.

2. **Preheat the Smoker**: Preheat your wood pellet smoker grill to 225°F (107°C) using your choice of wood pellets.

3. **Smoke the Ribs**: Place the ribs in the smoker. Smoke for about 3 hours, spraying them occasionally with a mix of honey and soy sauce to keep them moist.

4. **Wrap the Ribs**: Wrap the ribs in aluminum foil and return them to the smoker. Cook for another 2 hours.

5. **Finish and Serve**: Unwrap the ribs and place them back in the smoker for an additional hour, or until they reach an internal temperature of 195°F (90°C). Let them rest for 10 minutes before serving.

Macronutrients (per serving, approximate):

Calories: 580 kcal - **Carbohydrates:** 15g - **Protein:** 45g - **Fat:** 37g

BBQ SMOKED PORK STEAKS

Preparation Time: 15 minutes

Cooking Time: 2 hours

Servings: 4-6

Ingredients:

- 4 pork steaks (about 8 oz each)
- 1/4 cup barbecue sauce
- 2 tablespoons olive oil
- 2 tablespoons brown sugar
- 1 tablespoon paprika
- 1 teaspoon garlic powder
- 1 teaspoon onion powder
- Salt and pepper to taste
- Your choice of wood pellets for smoking (hickory or mesquite work well)

Directions:

1. **Prepare the Pork Steaks**: Rub each pork steak with olive oil. In a small bowl, mix together brown sugar, paprika, garlic powder, onion powder, salt, and pepper. Apply this rub evenly to the pork steaks.

2. **Preheat the Smoker**: Preheat your wood pellet smoker grill to 225°F (107°C) using your choice of wood pellets.

3. **Smoke the Pork Steaks**: Place the pork steaks on the smoker grate. Smoke for about 1.5 hours, or until they start to become tender.

4. **Glaze and Finish**: Brush the pork steaks with barbecue sauce and continue smoking for another 30 minutes, or until the internal temperature reaches 145°F (63°C).

5. **Rest and Serve**: Remove the pork steaks from the smoker and let them rest for 10 minutes before serving.

Macronutrients (per serving, approximate):

Calories: 400 kcal - **Carbohydrates:** 9g - **Protein:** 35g - **Fat:** 25g

SMOKED PORK BELLY BITES WITH BROWN SUGAR

Preparation Time: 15 minutes

Cooking Time: 3 hours

Servings: 6-8

Ingredients:

- 2 pounds pork belly, cut into 1-inch cubes
- 1/4 cup brown sugar
- 2 tablespoons honey
- 1 tablespoon soy sauce
- 2 teaspoons smoked paprika
- 1 teaspoon garlic powder
- 1 teaspoon onion powder
- Salt and pepper to taste
- Your choice of wood pellets for smoking (applewood or hickory work well)

Directions:

1. **Prepare the Pork Belly**: In a large bowl, combine the brown sugar, smoked paprika, garlic powder, onion powder, salt, and pepper. Add the pork belly cubes and toss to coat evenly.

2. **Preheat the Smoker**: Preheat your wood pellet smoker grill to 250°F (121°C) using your choice of wood pellets.

3. **Smoke the Pork Belly Bites**: Place the seasoned pork belly cubes on the smoker grate. Smoke for about 2.5 hours, or until they start to crisp on the outside.

4. **Glaze the Pork Belly**: In a small bowl, mix honey and soy sauce. Brush this mixture over the pork belly bites and continue smoking for another 30 minutes.

5. **Serve**: Once the pork belly bites are caramelized and tender, remove them from the smoker and serve.

Macronutrients (per serving, approximate):

Calories: 520 kcal - **Carbohydrates**: 10g - **Protein**: 14g - **Fat**: 46g

SMOKED ANDOUILLE SAUSAGE

Preparation Time: 10 minutes

Cooking Time: 2 hours

Servings: 6

Ingredients:

- 2 pounds Andouille sausage links
- 2 tablespoons olive oil
- 1 tablespoon Cajun seasoning
- Your choice of wood pellets for smoking (hickory or oak work well)

Directions:

1. **Prepare the Sausages**: Brush the Andouille sausage links with olive oil and evenly sprinkle them with Cajun seasoning.

2. **Preheat the Smoker**: Preheat your wood pellet smoker grill to 225°F (107°C) using your choice of wood pellets.

3. **Smoke the Sausages**: Place the seasoned Andouille sausages on the smoker grate. Smoke for about 2 hours, or until they are fully cooked and have a nice smoky flavor.

4. **Rest and Serve**: Remove the sausages from the smoker and let them rest for a few minutes. Slice and serve either as a main dish or as an addition to other dishes.

Macronutrients (per serving, approximate):

Calories: 350 kcal - **Carbohydrates**: 2g - **Protein**: 28g - **Fat**: 26g

SMOKED ST. LOUIS STYLE RIBS

Preparation Time: 20 minutes (plus overnight marinating)

Cooking Time: 5 hours

Servings: 4-6

Ingredients:

- 2 racks St. Louis style ribs (about 6 pounds)
- 1/4 cup apple cider vinegar
- 1/4 cup brown sugar
- 2 tablespoons paprika
- 1 tablespoon garlic powder
- 1 tablespoon onion powder
- 1 teaspoon cayenne pepper (optional for heat)
- 1 teaspoon black pepper
- 1 teaspoon salt
- Your choice of wood pellets for smoking (hickory or applewood work well)

Directions:

1. **Prepare the Ribs**: Remove the membrane from the back of the ribs. In a bowl, mix apple cider vinegar with brown sugar, paprika, garlic powder, onion powder, cayenne pepper, black pepper, and salt. Rub this mixture evenly over the ribs. Let the ribs marinate in the refrigerator overnight.

2. **Preheat the Smoker**: Preheat your wood pellet smoker grill to 225°F (107°C) using your choice of wood pellets.

3. **Smoke the Ribs**: Place the ribs in the smoker. Smoke for about 3 hours, spraying them occasionally with apple cider vinegar to keep them moist.

4. **Wrap the Ribs**: Wrap the ribs in aluminum foil and return them to the smoker. Cook for another 2 hours.

5. **Finish and Serve**: Unwrap the ribs and place them back in the smoker for an additional hour, or until they reach an internal temperature of 195°F (90°C). Let them rest for 10 minutes before serving.

Macronutrients (per serving, approximate):

Calories: 610 kcal - **Carbohydrates**: 12g - **Protein**: 46g - **Fat**: 42g

SMOKED PORK CARNITAS FOR TACOS

Preparation Time: 30 minutes

Cooking Time: 6 hours

Servings: 8

Ingredients:

- 4 pounds pork shoulder, cut into 2-inch chunks
- 1/4 cup orange juice
- 1/4 cup lime juice
- 4 cloves garlic, minced
- 2 teaspoons cumin
- 2 teaspoons oregano
- 1 teaspoon chili powder
- 1 teaspoon salt
- 1 teaspoon black pepper
- Your choice of wood pellets for smoking (applewood or mesquite work well)

Directions:

1. **Marinate the Pork**: In a large bowl, mix together orange juice, lime juice, minced garlic, cumin, oregano, chili powder, salt, and pepper. Add the pork chunks and toss to coat evenly. Let the pork marinate for about 20 minutes.

2. **Preheat the Smoker**: Preheat your wood pellet smoker grill to 250°F (121°C) using your choice of wood pellets.

3. **Smoke the Pork**: Place the marinated pork chunks on the smoker grate. Smoke for about 6 hours, or until the pork is tender and pulls apart easily.

4. **Crisp the Pork**: Optional - For added texture, transfer the smoked pork to a baking sheet and broil in the oven for a few minutes until the edges are crispy.

5. **Serve**: Shred the pork and serve as a filling for tacos, garnished with your favorite toppings such as diced onions, cilantro, and salsa.

Macronutrients (per serving, approximate):

Calories: 360 kcal - **Carbohydrates**: 3g - **Protein**: 48g - **Fat**: 18g

SMOKED PORK COUNTRY-STYLE RIBS

Preparation Time: 15 minutes

Cooking Time: 4 hours

Servings: 6

Ingredients:

- 3 pounds pork country-style ribs
- 1/4 cup barbecue sauce
- 2 tablespoons brown sugar
- 1 tablespoon smoked paprika
- 1 teaspoon garlic powder
- 1 teaspoon onion powder
- Salt and pepper to taste
- Your choice of wood pellets for smoking (hickory or applewood work well)

Directions:

1. **Prepare the Ribs**: In a bowl, combine brown sugar, smoked paprika, garlic powder, onion powder, salt, and pepper. Rub this mixture evenly over the ribs.

2. **Preheat the Smoker**: Preheat your wood pellet smoker grill to 225°F (107°C) using your choice of wood pellets.

3. **Smoke the Ribs**: Place the seasoned ribs on the smoker grate. Smoke for about 3 hours, or until they start to become tender.

4. **Glaze and Finish**: Brush the ribs with barbecue sauce and continue smoking for another hour, or until the internal temperature reaches 145°F (63°C).

5. **Rest and Serve**: Remove the ribs from the smoker and let them rest for 10 minutes before serving.

Macronutrients (per serving, approximate):

Calories: 400 kcal - **Carbohydrates:** 9g - **Protein:** 35g - **Fat:** 25g

CHAPTER 4
BEEF RECIPES

CLASSIC SMOKED BEEF BRISKET

 30 minutes (plus overnight resting)

 12 hours

 8-10

Ingredients:

- 1 whole beef brisket (about 10-12 pounds)
- 1/4 cup coarse salt
- 1/4 cup black pepper
- 2 tablespoons garlic powder
- 2 tablespoons onion powder
- 2 tablespoons smoked paprika
- 1 teaspoon cayenne pepper (optional for heat)
- Your choice of wood pellets for smoking (oak or hickory work well)

Directions:

1. **Prepare the Brisket**: Trim the fat on the brisket to about 1/4 inch thickness. In a bowl, mix together salt, black pepper, garlic powder, onion powder, smoked paprika, and cayenne pepper. Rub this mixture evenly all over the brisket. Let the brisket rest in the refrigerator overnight.

2. **Preheat the Smoker**: Preheat your wood pellet smoker grill to 225°F (107°C) using your choice of wood pellets.

3. **Smoke the Brisket**: Place the brisket on the smoker fat side up. Smoke for about 6 hours, until a nice bark forms on the surface.

4. **Wrap and Continue Smoking**: Wrap the brisket tightly in butcher paper or aluminum foil. Return it to the smoker and continue cooking for another 6 hours, or until the internal temperature reaches 200°F (93°C).

5. **Rest and Serve**: Remove the brisket from the smoker and let it rest for 1 hour before slicing against the grain and serving.

Macronutrients (per serving, approximate):

Calories: 480 kcal - **Carbohydrates:** 1g - **Protein:** 60g - **Fat:** 24g

HICKORY-SMOKED PRIME RIB

Preparation Time: 20 minutes (plus resting time)

Cooking Time: 6 hours

Servings: 8-10

Ingredients:

- 1 whole prime rib roast (about 10 pounds)
- 1/4 cup olive oil
- 1/4 cup kosher salt
- 2 tablespoons coarse black pepper
- 2 tablespoons garlic powder
- 2 tablespoons onion powder
- 1 tablespoon dried rosemary
- 1 tablespoon dried thyme
- Hickory wood pellets for smoking

Directions:

1. **Prepare the Prime Rib**: Rub the prime rib all over with olive oil. In a small bowl, mix together salt, black pepper, garlic powder, onion powder, rosemary, and thyme. Apply this rub evenly over the roast.

2. **Preheat the Smoker**: Preheat your wood pellet smoker grill to 225°F (107°C) using hickory wood pellets.

3. **Smoke the Prime Rib**: Place the prime rib on the smoker grate, fat side up. Smoke for about 6 hours, or until the internal temperature reaches 130°F (54°C) for medium-rare.

4. **Rest and Serve**: Remove the prime rib from the smoker and let it rest for 20-30 minutes. The temperature will continue to rise slightly during this time.

5. **Slice and Enjoy**: Carve the prime rib into thick slices and serve.

Macronutrients (per serving, approximate):

Calories: 750 kcal - **Carbohydrates**: 1g - **Protein**: 45g - **Fat**: 65g

SMOKED BEEF SHORT RIBS

Preparation Time: 15 minutes

Cooking Time: 8 hours

Servings: 6

Ingredients:

- 6 beef short ribs (about 5-6 pounds)
- 1/4 cup brown sugar
- 2 tablespoons kosher salt
- 2 tablespoons black pepper
- 1 tablespoon garlic powder
- 1 tablespoon onion powder
- 1 teaspoon smoked paprika
- 1 teaspoon cayenne pepper (optional for heat)
- Your choice of wood pellets for smoking (oak or cherry work well)

Directions:

1. **Prepare the Short Ribs**: In a small bowl, mix together brown sugar, salt, black pepper, garlic powder, onion powder, smoked paprika, and cayenne pepper. Rub this mixture evenly over the short ribs.

2. **Preheat the Smoker**: Preheat your wood pellet smoker grill to 225°F (107°C) using your choice of wood pellets.

3. **Smoke the Short Ribs**: Place the short ribs on the smoker grate. Smoke for about 6 hours, or until they develop a deep, dark bark.

4. **Wrap and Continue Cooking**: Wrap the short ribs in butcher paper or aluminum foil and return them to the smoker. Continue cooking for another 2 hours, or until the ribs are tender and the internal temperature reaches around 200°F (93°C).

5. **Rest and Serve**: Remove the short ribs from the smoker and let them rest for at least 30 minutes before serving.

Macronutrients (per serving, approximate):

Calories: 680 kcal - **Carbohydrates**: 8g - **Protein**: 48g - **Fat**: 50g

TEXAS-STYLE SMOKED BEEF SAUSAGE

Preparation Time: 20 minutes

Cooking Time: 3 hours

Servings: 6

Ingredients:

- 2 pounds beef sausage links
- 1/4 cup mustard
- 2 tablespoons Worcestershire sauce
- 1 tablespoon garlic powder
- 1 tablespoon onion powder
- 1 teaspoon smoked paprika
- Salt and pepper to taste
- Your choice of wood pellets for smoking (hickory or mesquite work well)

Directions:

1. **Prepare the Sausages**: In a small bowl, mix together mustard, Worcestershire sauce, garlic powder, onion powder, smoked paprika, salt, and pepper. Brush this mixture over the beef sausage links.

2. **Preheat the Smoker**: Preheat your wood pellet smoker grill to 225°F (107°C) using your choice of wood pellets.

3. **Smoke the Sausages**: Place the sausages on the smoker grate. Smoke for about 3 hours, or until they have a deep, rich color and are cooked through.

4. **Rest and Serve**: Remove the sausages from the smoker and let them rest for a few minutes. Slice and serve.

Macronutrients (per serving, approximate):

Calories: 360 kcal - **Carbohydrates**: 3g - **Protein**: 20g - **Fat**: 30g

APPLEWOOD SMOKED TRI-TIP

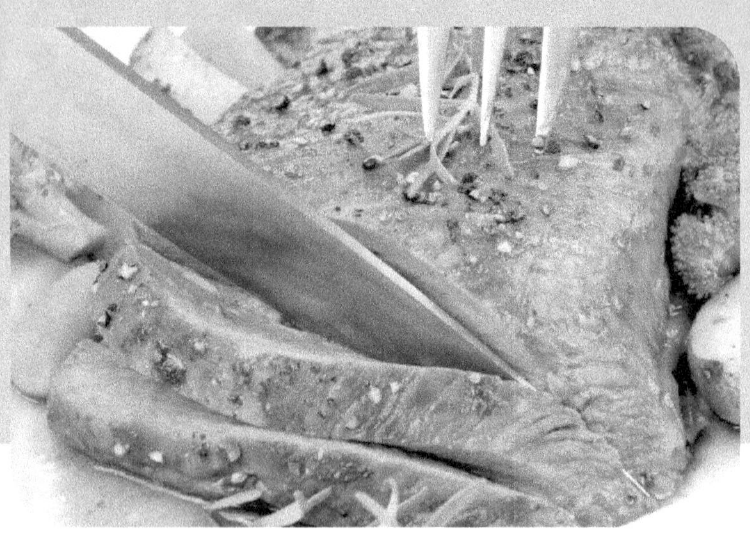

Preparation Time: 15 minutes (plus 2 hours for marinating)

Cooking Time: 2 hours

Servings: 4-6

Ingredients:

- 1 tri-tip roast (about 2-3 pounds)
- 1/4 cup soy sauce
- 1/4 cup apple cider vinegar
- 2 tablespoons olive oil
- 2 tablespoons brown sugar
- 1 tablespoon garlic powder
- 1 tablespoon onion powder
- 1 teaspoon black pepper
- 1 teaspoon smoked paprika
- Applewood pellets for smoking

Directions:

1. **Marinate the Tri-Tip**: In a large bowl, whisk together soy sauce, apple cider vinegar, olive oil, brown sugar, garlic powder, onion powder, black pepper, and smoked paprika. Place the tri-tip in the marinade, ensuring it is well-coated. Cover and refrigerate for at least 2 hours.

2. **Preheat the Smoker**: Preheat your wood pellet smoker grill to 250°F (121°C) using applewood pellets.

3. **Smoke the Tri-Tip**: Remove the tri-tip from the marinade and place it on the smoker grate. Smoke for about 2 hours, or until the internal temperature reaches 135°F (57°C) for medium-rare.

4. **Rest and Slice**: Remove the tri-tip from the smoker and let it rest for 10-15 minutes. Slice against the grain and serve.

Macronutrients (per serving, approximate):

Calories: 400 kcal - **Carbohydrates:** 5g - **Protein:** 45g - **Fat:** 22g

MESQUITE SMOKED T-BONE STEAKS

Preparation Time: 10 minutes (plus 1 hour for coming to room temperature)

Cooking Time: 1 hour

Servings: 4

Ingredients:

- 4 T-bone steaks (about 1 inch thick)
- 2 tablespoons olive oil
- 2 tablespoons coarse salt
- 2 tablespoons black pepper
- 1 tablespoon garlic powder
- 1 tablespoon onion powder
- Mesquite wood pellets for smoking

Directions:

1. **Prepare the Steaks**: Rub each steak with olive oil. In a small bowl, mix together salt, black pepper, garlic powder, and onion powder. Season the steaks evenly with this mixture. Allow the steaks to sit at room temperature for about 1 hour before smoking.

2. **Preheat the Smoker**: Preheat your wood pellet smoker grill to 225°F (107°C) using mesquite wood pellets.

3. **Smoke the T-Bone Steaks**: Place the seasoned steaks on the smoker grate. Smoke for about 1 hour, or until the internal temperature reaches 130°F (54°C) for medium-rare.

4. **Rest and Serve**: Remove the steaks from the smoker and let them rest for 10 minutes. This allows the juices to redistribute throughout the meat.

Macronutrients (per serving, approximate):

Calories: 520 kcal - **Carbohydrates**: 1g - **Protein**: 45g - **Fat**: 36g

SMOKED BEEF TENDERLOIN

Preparation Time: 20 minutes (plus resting time)

Cooking Time: 2.5 hours

Servings: 6

Ingredients:

- 1 whole beef tenderloin (about 3-4 pounds)
- 2 tablespoons olive oil
- 2 tablespoons coarse salt
- 1 tablespoon cracked black pepper
- 1 tablespoon garlic powder
- 1 tablespoon rosemary, finely chopped
- Your choice of wood pellets for smoking (oak or cherry work well)

Directions:

1. **Prepare the Beef Tenderloin**: Trim any excess fat from the tenderloin. Rub it all over with olive oil. In a small bowl, mix together salt, black pepper, garlic powder, and rosemary. Apply this seasoning evenly over the tenderloin.

2. **Preheat the Smoker**: Preheat your wood pellet smoker grill to 225°F (107°C) using your choice of wood pellets.

3. **Smoke the Beef Tenderloin**: Place the seasoned beef tenderloin on the smoker grate. Smoke for about 2.5 hours, or until the internal temperature reaches 130°F (54°C) for medium-rare.

4. **Rest and Slice**: Remove the beef tenderloin from the smoker and let it rest for 15-20 minutes. Slice into medallions and serve.

Macronutrients (per serving, approximate):

Calories: 410 kcal - **Carbohydrates:** 1g - **Protein:** 40g - **Fat:** 27g

BOURBON BARREL SMOKED BURGERS

Preparation Time: 20 minutes

Cooking Time: 1 hour

Servings: 6

Ingredients:

- 2 pounds ground beef (80/20 lean-to-fat ratio)
- 1/4 cup bourbon (optional, for flavor)
- 1 tablespoon Worcestershire sauce
- 1 teaspoon garlic powder
- 1 teaspoon onion powder
- 1 teaspoon smoked paprika
- Salt and pepper to taste
- 6 burger buns
- Toppings as desired (lettuce, tomato, cheese, etc.)
- Your choice of wood pellets for smoking (oak or hickory work well)

Directions:

1. **Prepare the Burger Patties**: In a large bowl, mix together ground beef, bourbon, Worcestershire sauce, garlic powder, onion powder, smoked paprika, salt, and pepper. Form into 6 equal-sized patties.

2. **Preheat the Smoker**: Preheat your wood pellet smoker grill to 225°F (107°C) using your choice of wood pellets.

3. **Smoke the Burgers**: Place the burger patties on the smoker grate. Smoke for about 1 hour, or until they reach an internal temperature of 160°F (71°C) for well-done.

4. **Toast the Buns**: During the last few minutes of cooking, place the burger buns on the smoker to lightly toast them.

5. **Assemble and Serve**: Place each burger on a bun and add your desired toppings.

Macronutrients (per serving, approximate):

Calories: 510 kcal - **Carbohydrates**: 23g (excluding additional toppings)
Protein: 32g - **Fat**: 31g

SMOKED CHUCK ROAST

Ingredients:

- 1 chuck roast (about 3-4 pounds)
- 2 tablespoons olive oil
- 2 tablespoons coarse salt
- 2 tablespoons ground black pepper
- 1 tablespoon garlic powder
- 1 tablespoon onion powder
- 1 teaspoon smoked paprika
- Your choice of wood pellets for smoking (hickory or oak work well)

Directions:

1. **Prepare the Chuck Roast**: Rub the chuck roast all over with olive oil. In a small bowl, mix together salt, black pepper, garlic powder, onion powder, and smoked paprika. Apply this rub evenly over the roast.

2. **Preheat the Smoker**: Preheat your wood pellet smoker grill to 225°F (107°C) using your choice of wood pellets.

3. **Smoke the Chuck Roast**: Place the seasoned chuck roast on the smoker grate. Smoke for about 8 hours, or until the internal temperature reaches 190°F (88°C) for a tender, pull-apart texture.

4. **Rest and Serve**: Remove the chuck roast from the smoker and let it rest for 20-30 minutes before slicing or shredding.

Macronutrients (per serving, approximate):

Calories: 450 kcal - **Carbohydrates**: 1g - **Protein**: 38g - **Fat**: 32g

SMOKED BEEF RIBEYE ROAST

Preparation Time: 15 minutes (plus resting time)

Cooking Time: 3 to 4 hours

Servings: 6-8

Ingredients:

- 1 whole ribeye roast (about 5-6 pounds)
- 2 tablespoons olive oil
- 1/4 cup coarse sea salt
- 2 tablespoons ground black pepper
- 2 tablespoons garlic powder
- 1 tablespoon onion powder
- 1 tablespoon dried thyme
- Your choice of wood pellets for smoking (oak or cherry work well)

Directions:

1. **Prepare the Ribeye Roast**: Coat the ribeye roast with olive oil. In a small bowl, mix together sea salt, black pepper, garlic powder, onion powder, and thyme. Rub this seasoning blend evenly over the entire roast.

2. **Preheat the Smoker**: Preheat your wood pellet smoker grill to 250°F (121°C) using your choice of wood pellets.

3. **Smoke the Ribeye Roast**: Place the seasoned ribeye roast on the smoker grate. Smoke for about 3 to 4 hours, or until the internal temperature reaches 130°F (54°C) for medium-rare.

4. **Rest and Carve**: Remove the ribeye roast from the smoker and let it rest for at least 20 minutes before carving into slices.

Macronutrients (per serving, approximate):

Calories: 650 kcal - **Carbohydrates:** 1g - **Protein:** 58g - **Fat:** 45g

GARLIC BUTTER SMOKED SIRLOIN STEAK

Preparation Time: 15 minutes

Cooking Time: 1.5 hours

Servings: 4

Ingredients:

- 4 sirloin steaks (about 8 oz each)
- 2 tablespoons olive oil
- Salt and pepper to taste
- 4 tablespoons butter
- 2 cloves garlic, minced
- 1 tablespoon fresh parsley, chopped
- Your choice of wood pellets for smoking (hickory or mesquite work well)

Directions:

1. **Prepare the Steaks**: Rub each sirloin steak with olive oil and season generously with salt and pepper.

2. **Preheat the Smoker**: Preheat your wood pellet smoker grill to 225°F (107°C) using your choice of wood pellets.

3. **Smoke the Sirloin Steaks**: Place the seasoned steaks on the smoker grate. Smoke for about 1.5 hours, or until the internal temperature reaches 135°F (57°C) for medium-rare.

4. **Make Garlic Butter**: While the steaks are smoking, melt the butter in a small saucepan. Add minced garlic and parsley, and cook for 1-2 minutes until fragrant. Keep warm.

5. **Serve**: Once the steaks reach the desired doneness, remove them from the smoker. Top each steak with a spoonful of the garlic butter and let rest for 5 minutes before serving.

Macronutrients (per serving, approximate):

Calories: 550 kcal - **Carbohydrates**: 1g - **Protein**: 45g - **Fat**: 40g

OAK-SMOKED FLANK STEAK

Preparation Time: 25 minutes (plus 2 hours for marinating)

Cooking Time: 1.5 hours

Servings: 4-6

Ingredients:

- 2 pounds flank steak
- 1/4 cup soy sauce
- 1/4 cup olive oil
- 3 tablespoons balsamic vinegar
- 2 tablespoons honey
- 2 cloves garlic, minced
- 1 teaspoon ground black pepper
- 1 teaspoon smoked paprika
- Oak wood pellets for smoking

Directions:

1. **Marinate the Flank Steak**: In a bowl, whisk together soy sauce, olive oil, balsamic vinegar, honey, minced garlic, black pepper, and smoked paprika. Place the flank steak in a large resealable bag and pour the marinade over it. Ensure the steak is well-coated, seal the bag, and marinate in the refrigerator for at least 2 hours.

2. **Preheat the Smoker**: Preheat your wood pellet smoker grill to 225°F (107°C) using oak wood pellets.

3. **Smoke the Flank Steak**: Remove the steak from the marinade and place it on the smoker grate. Discard the remaining marinade. Smoke for about 1.5 hours, or until the internal temperature reaches 130°F (54°C) for medium-rare.

4. **Rest and Slice**: Remove the steak from the smoker and let it rest for 10 minutes. Slice against the grain into thin strips.

Macronutrients (per serving, approximate):

Calories: 400 kcal - **Carbohydrates**: 8g - **Protein**: 40g - **Fat**: 22g

SMOKED BEEF BACK RIBS

Preparation Time: 15 minutes

Cooking Time: 6 hours

Servings: 4-6

Ingredients:

- 2 racks of beef back ribs (about 6-7 pounds)
- 1/4 cup brown sugar
- 2 tablespoons coarse salt
- 2 tablespoons ground black pepper
- 1 tablespoon garlic powder
- 1 tablespoon onion powder
- 1 teaspoon smoked paprika
- 1 teaspoon cayenne pepper (optional for heat)
- Your choice of wood pellets for smoking (hickory or mesquite work well)

Directions:

1. **Prepare the Ribs**: Remove the membrane from the back of the ribs. In a bowl, mix together brown sugar, salt, black pepper, garlic powder, onion powder, smoked paprika, and cayenne pepper. Rub this mixture evenly over the ribs.

2. **Preheat the Smoker**: Preheat your wood pellet smoker grill to 225°F (107°C) using your choice of wood pellets.

3. **Smoke the Ribs**: Place the seasoned ribs on the smoker grate. Smoke for about 6 hours, or until the ribs are tender and the meat easily pulls away from the bone.

4. **Rest and Serve**: Remove the ribs from the smoker and let them rest for 10-15 minutes before serving.

Macronutrients (per serving, approximate):

- **Calories**: 560 kcal - **Carbohydrates**: 10g - **Protein**: 45g - **Fat**: 37g

SMOKED BEEF SHANK OSSO BUCO

Preparation Time: 20 minutes

Cooking Time: 6 hours

Servings: 4

Ingredients:

- 4 beef shanks (about 1 inch thick each)
- 2 tablespoons olive oil
- 1/4 cup all-purpose flour
- Salt and pepper to taste
- 1 onion, chopped
- 2 carrots, chopped
- 2 celery stalks, chopped
- 4 cloves garlic, minced
- 1 cup red wine
- 2 cups beef broth
- 1 tablespoon tomato paste
- 1 teaspoon dried thyme
- 1 bay leaf
- Your choice of wood pellets for smoking (oak or hickory work well)

Directions:

1. **Prepare the Beef Shanks:** Season the beef shanks with salt and pepper, then dredge them in flour. Heat olive oil in a skillet over medium heat and brown the shanks on both sides. Transfer to a plate.

2. **Preheat the Smoker:** Preheat your wood pellet smoker grill to 225°F (107°C) using your choice of wood pellets.

3. **Prepare the Braising Liquid:** In the same skillet, add onion, carrots, celery, and garlic. Cook until softened. Stir in red wine, beef broth, tomato paste, thyme, and bay leaf. Bring to a simmer.

4. **Smoke the Beef Shanks:** Place the beef shanks on the smoker grate. Carefully pour the braising liquid over the shanks. Smoke for about 6 hours, or until the meat is tender and falling off the bone.

5. **Serve:** Remove the beef shanks and vegetables from the smoker. Discard the bay leaf. Serve the shanks with the vegetables and sauce.

Macronutrients (per serving, approximate):

Calories: 450 kcal - **Carbohydrates:** 15g - **Protein:** 40g - **Fat:** 20g

JALAPEÑO CHEDDAR SMOKED MEATLOAF

Preparation Time: 20 minutes

Cooking Time: 3 hours

Servings: 6

Ingredients:

- 2 pounds ground beef (80/20 lean-to-fat ratio)
- 1 cup sharp cheddar cheese, shredded
- 2 jalapeños, finely chopped (remove seeds for less heat)
- 1/2 cup breadcrumbs
- 1/4 cup milk
- 1 egg
- 1 onion, finely chopped
- 2 cloves garlic, minced
- 2 tablespoons Worcestershire sauce
- 1 teaspoon salt
- 1 teaspoon black pepper
- For the glaze: 1/2 cup ketchup, 2 tablespoons brown sugar, 1 tablespoon apple cider vinegar
- Your choice of wood pellets for smoking (hickory or mesquite work well)

Directions:

1. **Prepare the Meatloaf Mixture**: In a large bowl, combine ground beef, cheddar cheese, jalapeños, breadcrumbs, milk, egg, onion, garlic, Worcestershire sauce, salt, and pepper. Mix until well combined but avoid overmixing.

2. **Form the Meatloaf**: Shape the mixture into a loaf on a sheet of aluminum foil or a baking sheet.

3. **Preheat the Smoker**: Preheat your wood pellet smoker grill to 250°F (121°C) using your choice of wood pellets.

4. **Smoke the Meatloaf**: Place the meatloaf on the smoker grate. Smoke for about 3 hours, or until the internal temperature reaches 160°F (71°C).

5. **Glaze and Serve**: In the last 30 minutes of smoking, mix together ketchup, brown sugar, and apple cider vinegar. Brush this glaze over the meatloaf. Serve the meatloaf sliced.

Macronutrients (per serving, approximate):

Calories: 500 kcal - **Carbohydrates:** 15g - **Protein:** 35g - **Fat:** 32g

SMOKED SKIRT STEAK FAJITAS

Preparation Time: 25 minutes (plus 1 hour for marinating)

Cooking Time: 1 hour

Servings: 4-6

Ingredients:

- 2 pounds skirt steak
- 1/4 cup olive oil
- Juice of 2 limes
- 3 cloves garlic, minced
- 1 tablespoon chili powder
- 1 teaspoon cumin
- 1 teaspoon smoked paprika
- Salt and pepper to taste
- 2 bell peppers, sliced
- 1 large onion, sliced
- Tortillas and fajita toppings (sour cream, guacamole, salsa, etc.)
- Your choice of wood pellets for smoking (mesquite or hickory work well)

Directions:

1. **Marinate the Skirt Steak**: In a bowl, whisk together olive oil, lime juice, garlic, chili powder, cumin, smoked paprika, salt, and pepper. Place the skirt steak in a resealable bag and pour the marinade over it. Marinate in the refrigerator for at least 1 hour.

2. **Preheat the Smoker**: Preheat your wood pellet smoker grill to 225°F (107°C) using your choice of wood pellets.

3. **Smoke the Skirt Steak and Vegetables**: Place the marinated skirt steak and sliced bell peppers and onion on the smoker grate. Smoke for about 1 hour, or until the steak reaches your desired doneness and the vegetables are tender.

4. **Rest and Slice the Steak**: Remove the steak from the smoker and let it rest for 10 minutes. Slice the steak against the grain into thin strips.

5. **Serve**: Serve the sliced steak and smoked vegetables with warm tortillas and your choice of fajita toppings.

Macronutrients (per serving, approximate):

Calories: 500 kcal - **Carbohydrates**: 15g (excluding tortillas and toppings)
Protein: 45g - **Fat**: 28g

CHERRY WOOD SMOKED BRISKET BURNT ENDS

Preparation Time: 30 minutes (plus overnight resting)

Cooking Time: 10 hours

Servings: 6-8

Ingredients:

- 1 whole packer brisket (about 12-14 pounds)
- 1/4 cup brown sugar
- 1/4 cup paprika
- 2 tablespoons coarse salt
- 2 tablespoons black pepper
- 1 tablespoon garlic powder
- 1 tablespoon onion powder
- 1 teaspoon cayenne pepper (optional for heat)
- Cherry wood pellets for smoking

Directions:

1. **Prepare the Brisket**: Trim the fat on the brisket to about 1/4 inch thickness. Mix together brown sugar, paprika, salt, black pepper, garlic powder, onion powder, and cayenne pepper. Rub this mixture evenly over the brisket. Let the brisket rest in the refrigerator overnight.

2. **Preheat the Smoker**: Preheat your wood pellet smoker grill to 225°F (107°C) using cherry wood pellets.

3. **Smoke the Brisket**: Place the brisket on the smoker fat side up. Smoke for about 8 hours, or until it develops a deep, dark bark and the internal temperature reaches 165°F (74°C).

4. **Make Burnt Ends**: Remove the brisket and cut the point section into 1-inch cubes. Toss the cubes with additional rub and a bit of barbecue sauce, then return them to the smoker. Smoke for another 2 hours, or until they are caramelized and tender.

5. **Rest and Serve**: Let the burnt ends rest for 15-20 minutes before serving.

Macronutrients (per serving, approximate):

Calories: 650 kcal - **Carbohydrates**: 10g - **Protein**: 60g - **Fat**: 40g

SMOKED LONDON BROIL

Preparation Time: 20 minutes (plus 4 hours for marinating)

Cooking Time: 1.5 hours

Servings: 4-6

Ingredients:

- 1 London broil (about 2-3 pounds)
- 1/4 cup soy sauce
- 1/4 cup balsamic vinegar
- 2 tablespoons olive oil
- 2 tablespoons Worcestershire sauce
- 2 cloves garlic, minced
- 1 tablespoon brown sugar
- 1 teaspoon dried rosemary
- 1 teaspoon dried thyme
- 1 teaspoon black pepper
- Your choice of wood pellets for smoking (oak or hickory work well)

Directions:

1. **Marinate the London Broil**: In a bowl, whisk together soy sauce, balsamic vinegar, olive oil, Worcestershire sauce, minced garlic, brown sugar, rosemary, thyme, and black pepper. Place the London broil in a resealable bag and pour the marinade over it. Marinate in the refrigerator for at least 4 hours, preferably overnight.

2. **Preheat the Smoker**: Preheat your wood pellet smoker grill to 225°F (107°C) using your choice of wood pellets.

3. **Smoke the London Broil**: Remove the London broil from the marinade and place it on the smoker grate. Smoke for about 1.5 hours, or until the internal temperature reaches 135°F (57°C) for medium-rare.

4. **Rest and Slice**: Remove the London broil from the smoker and let it rest for 10 minutes. Slice against the grain into thin strips.

Macronutrients (per serving, approximate):

Calories: 300 kcal - **Carbohydrates**: 5g - **Protein**: 40g - **Fat**: 12g

SMOKED PASTRAMI

Preparation Time: 30 minutes (plus curing time of 4-7 days)

Cooking Time: 6-8 hours

Servings: 8-10

Ingredients:

- 1 beef brisket flat (4-5 pounds)
- For the brine:
- 1 gallon water
- 1 cup kosher salt
- 1/2 cup sugar
- 1/4 cup pickling spices
- 5 cloves garlic, minced
- 1 teaspoon pink curing salt (Prague Powder #1)
- For the rub:
- 1/4 cup coarsely ground black pepper
- 1/4 cup coriander powder
- 1 tablespoon paprika
- 1 tablespoon garlic powder
- 1 tablespoon onion powder
- Your choice of wood pellets for smoking (hickory or oak work well)

Directions:

1. **Cure the Brisket**: Combine all brine ingredients in a large pot and bring to a boil. Let cool completely. Place the brisket in the brine, ensuring it is fully submerged. Cure in the refrigerator for 4-7 days.

2. **Prepare for Smoking**: Remove the brisket from the brine and rinse thoroughly. Pat dry. Mix together the rub ingredients and coat the brisket evenly on all sides.

3. **Preheat the Smoker**: Preheat your wood pellet smoker grill to 225°F (107°C) using your choice of wood pellets.

4. **Smoke the Pastrami**: Place the brisket on the smoker grate. Smoke for about 6-8 hours, or until the internal temperature reaches 190°F (88°C).

5. **Rest and Slice**: Remove the pastrami from the smoker and let it rest for 1 hour. Slice thinly against the grain.

Macronutrients (per serving, approximate):

Calories: 350 kcal - **Carbohydrates**: 3g - **Protein**: 50g - **Fat**: 15g

SMOKED BEEF TOP ROUND FOR SANDWICHES

Preparation Time: 15 minutes

Cooking Time: 6 hours

Servings: 6-8

Ingredients:

- 1 beef top round roast (about 3-4 pounds)
- 2 tablespoons olive oil
- 2 tablespoons coarse salt
- 1 tablespoon black pepper
- 1 tablespoon garlic powder
- 1 tablespoon onion powder
- 1 teaspoon dried thyme
- Your choice of wood pellets for smoking (oak or hickory work well)

Directions:

1. **Prepare the Beef Top Round**: Coat the beef top round roast with olive oil. In a small bowl, combine salt, black pepper, garlic powder, onion powder, and thyme. Rub this mixture evenly over the roast.

2. **Preheat the Smoker**: Preheat your wood pellet smoker grill to 225°F (107°C) using your choice of wood pellets.

3. **Smoke the Beef Top Round**: Place the seasoned roast on the smoker grate. Smoke for about 6 hours, or until the internal temperature reaches 145°F (63°C) for medium-rare.

4. **Rest and Slice**: Remove the roast from the smoker and let it rest for 20 minutes. Slice thinly against the grain.

Macronutrients (per serving, approximate):

Calories: 300 kcal - **Carbohydrates:** 1g - **Protein:** 50g - **Fat:** 10g

PECAN WOOD SMOKED BEEF PLATE RIBS

Preparation Time: 20 minutes

Cooking Time: 6 hours

Servings: 4-6

Ingredients:

- 3 large beef plate ribs (about 6-7 pounds)
- 2 tablespoons olive oil
- 1/4 cup coarse salt
- 1/4 cup black pepper
- 1 tablespoon garlic powder
- 1 tablespoon onion powder
- Pecan wood pellets for smoking

Directions:

1. **Prepare the Ribs**: Rub the beef plate ribs all over with olive oil. In a small bowl, mix together salt, black pepper, garlic powder, and onion powder. Apply this rub evenly over the ribs.

2. **Preheat the Smoker**: Preheat your wood pellet smoker grill to 250°F (121°C) using pecan wood pellets.

3. **Smoke the Ribs**: Place the seasoned ribs on the smoker grate, bone side down. Smoke for about 6 hours, or until the meat is tender and pulls back from the bone, typically reaching an internal temperature of around 200°F (93°C).

4. **Rest and Serve**: Remove the ribs from the smoker and let them rest for 20-30 minutes. Slice between the bones and serve.

Macronutrients (per serving, approximate):

Calories: 620 kcal - **Carbohydrates:** 1g - **Protein:** 45g - **Fat:** 48g

SMOKED FILET MIGNON

Preparation Time: 15 minutes

Cooking Time: 1 hour

Servings: 4

Ingredients:

- 4 filet mignon steaks (about 6-8 ounces each)
- 2 tablespoons olive oil
- 2 tablespoons coarse salt
- 1 tablespoon cracked black pepper
- 1 tablespoon garlic powder
- 1 teaspoon dried rosemary
- Your choice of wood pellets for smoking (applewood or cherry work well)

Directions:

1. **Prepare the Filet Mignon**: Rub each filet mignon steak with olive oil. In a small bowl, combine salt, cracked black pepper, garlic powder, and dried rosemary. Apply this seasoning evenly to each steak.

2. **Preheat the Smoker**: Preheat your wood pellet smoker grill to 225°F (107°C) using your choice of wood pellets.

3. **Smoke the Filet Mignon**: Place the seasoned steaks on the smoker grate. Smoke for about 1 hour, or until the internal temperature reaches 130°F (54°C) for medium-rare.

4. **Rest and Serve**: Remove the steaks from the smoker and let them rest for 10 minutes. This allows the juices to redistribute throughout the meat.

Macronutrients (per serving, approximate):

Calories: 360 kcal - **Carbohydrates:** 1g - **Protein:** 45g - **Fat:** 20g

ESPRESSO RUBBED SMOKED BRISKET

Preparation Time: 30 minutes (plus overnight resting)

Cooking Time: 10 hours

Servings: 8-10

Ingredients:

- 1 whole beef brisket (about 10-12 pounds)
- 2 tablespoons finely ground espresso beans
- 2 tablespoons brown sugar
- 2 tablespoons smoked paprika
- 1 tablespoon coarse salt
- 1 tablespoon black pepper
- 1 tablespoon garlic powder
- 1 tablespoon onion powder
- 1 teaspoon cayenne pepper (optional for heat)
- Your choice of wood pellets for smoking (oak or hickory work well)

Directions:

1. **Prepare the Brisket**: Trim the fat on the brisket to about 1/4 inch thickness. In a bowl, mix together espresso grounds, brown sugar, smoked paprika, salt, black pepper, garlic powder, onion powder, and cayenne pepper. Rub this mixture evenly over the brisket. Let the brisket rest in the refrigerator overnight.

2. **Preheat the Smoker**: Preheat your wood pellet smoker grill to 225°F (107°C) using your choice of wood pellets.

3. **Smoke the Brisket**: Place the brisket on the smoker fat side up. Smoke for about 10 hours, or until it develops a deep, dark bark and the internal temperature reaches around 200°F (93°C).

4. **Rest and Serve**: Remove the brisket from the smoker and let it rest for 1 hour. Slice against the grain and serve.

Macronutrients (per serving, approximate):

Calories: 650 kcal - **Carbohydrates:** 3g - **Protein:** 60g - **Fat:** 42g

CHAPTER 5
CHICKEN RECIPES

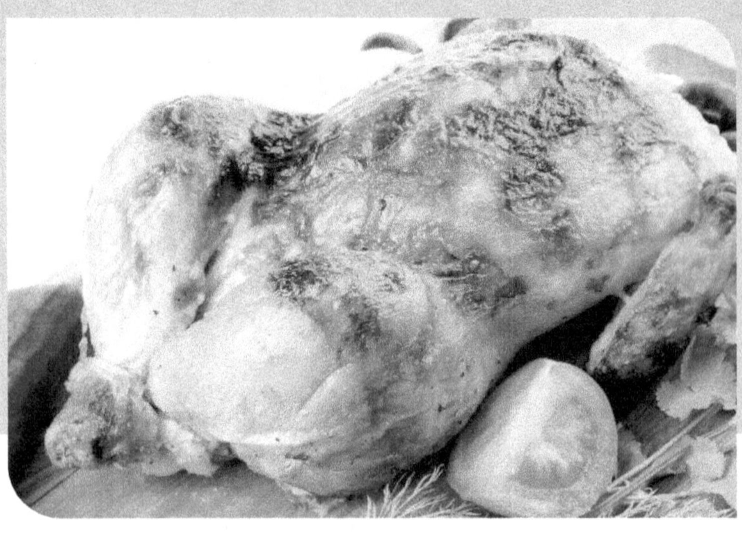

APPLEWOOD SMOKED WHOLE CHICKEN

Preparation Time: 20 minutes (plus overnight brining)

Cooking Time: 3 hours

Servings: 4-6

Ingredients:

- 1 whole chicken (about 4-5 pounds)
- For the brine:
  - 1 gallon water
  - 1/2 cup kosher salt
  - 1/2 cup brown sugar
  - 2 tablespoons apple cider vinegar
  - 1 tablespoon black peppercorns
  - 2 bay leaves
- For the rub:
  - 2 tablespoons olive oil
  - 1 tablespoon smoked paprika
  - 1 teaspoon garlic powder
  - 1 teaspoon onion powder
  - 1 teaspoon dried thyme
  - Salt and pepper to taste
- Applewood pellets for smoking

Directions:

1. **Brine the Chicken**: Combine all brine ingredients in a large pot and bring to a simmer until salt and sugar are dissolved. Cool completely. Submerge the chicken in the brine and refrigerate overnight.

2. **Preheat the Smoker**: Preheat your wood pellet smoker grill to 250°F (121°C) using applewood pellets.

3. **Prepare the Chicken**: Remove the chicken from the brine, rinse, and pat dry. Mix the rub ingredients and coat the chicken evenly. Drizzle with olive oil.

4. **Smoke the Chicken**: Place the chicken on the smoker grate. Smoke for about 3 hours, or until the internal temperature in the thickest part of the chicken reaches 165°F (74°C).

5. **Rest and Serve**: Let the chicken rest for 10 minutes before carving.

Macronutrients (per serving, approximate):

Calories: 400 kcal - **Carbohydrates**: 1g - **Protein**: 35g - **Fat**: 28g

HICKORY SMOKED CHICKEN WINGS

Preparation Time: 15 minutes (plus marinating time)

Cooking Time: 2 hours

Servings: 4-6

Ingredients:

- 3 pounds chicken wings, separated into drumettes and flats
- For the marinade:
  - 1/2 cup soy sauce
  - 1/4 cup olive oil
  - 1/4 cup honey
  - 2 cloves garlic, minced
  - 1 teaspoon smoked paprika
  - 1 teaspoon garlic powder
  - 1/2 teaspoon cayenne pepper (optional, for heat)
- Hickory wood pellets for smoking

Directions:

1. **Marinate the Wings**: In a large bowl, whisk together the soy sauce, olive oil, honey, minced garlic, smoked paprika, garlic powder, and cayenne pepper. Add the chicken wings and toss to coat evenly. Cover and marinate in the refrigerator for at least 2 hours, preferably overnight.

2. **Preheat the Smoker**: Preheat your wood pellet smoker grill to 250°F (121°C) using hickory wood pellets.

3. **Smoke the Wings**: Remove the wings from the marinade and place them on the smoker grate. Smoke for about 2 hours, or until the wings are golden brown and the internal temperature reaches 165°F (74°C).

4. **Crisp the Wings** (Optional): If you prefer crisper skin, increase the smoker temperature to 375°F (190°C) during the last 30 minutes of cooking.

5. **Serve**: Remove the wings from the smoker and let them rest for a few minutes. Serve hot with your choice of dipping sauces or enjoy them as they are.

Macronutrients (per serving, approximate):

Calories: 410 kcal - **Carbohydrates:** 11g - **Protein:** 35g - **Fat:** 24g

MESQUITE SMOKED CHICKEN THIGHS

Preparation Time: 15 minutes (plus optional marinating time)

Cooking Time: 1.5 hours

Servings: 4-6

Ingredients:

- 8 chicken thighs, bone-in and skin-on
- 1/4 cup olive oil
- 2 tablespoons honey
- 2 tablespoons soy sauce
- 1 tablespoon apple cider vinegar
- 2 cloves garlic, minced
- 1 teaspoon smoked paprika
- 1 teaspoon garlic powder
- 1 teaspoon onion powder
- Salt and pepper to taste
- Mesquite wood pellets for smoking

Directions:

1. **Prepare the Chicken**: In a bowl, whisk together olive oil, honey, soy sauce, apple cider vinegar, minced garlic, smoked paprika, garlic powder, onion powder, salt, and pepper. Coat the chicken thighs in the mixture. For more flavor, marinate in the refrigerator for 1-2 hours (optional).

2. **Preheat the Smoker**: Preheat your wood pellet smoker grill to 250°F (121°C) using mesquite wood pellets.

3. **Smoke the Chicken Thighs**: Place the chicken thighs on the smoker grate, skin side up. Smoke for about 1.5 hours, or until the internal temperature reaches 165°F (74°C) and the skin is crispy.

4. **Rest and Serve**: Remove the chicken thighs from the smoker and let them rest for a few minutes before serving.

Macronutrients (per serving, approximate):

Calories: 400 kcal - **Carbohydrates**: 5g - **Protein**: 30g - **Fat**: 29g

SMOKED CHICKEN BREAST WITH HERB RUB

Preparation Time: 15 minutes

Cooking Time: 1.5 hours

Servings: 4

Ingredients:

- 4 boneless, skinless chicken breasts
- 2 tablespoons olive oil
- For the rub:
  - 1 tablespoon dried rosemary
  - 1 tablespoon dried thyme
  - 1 teaspoon garlic powder
  - 1 teaspoon onion powder
  - 1 teaspoon smoked paprika
  - Salt and pepper to taste
- Your choice of wood pellets for smoking (applewood or cherry work well)

Directions:

1. **Prepare the Chicken**: Coat the chicken breasts with olive oil. In a small bowl, mix together the rosemary, thyme, garlic powder, onion powder, smoked paprika, salt, and pepper. Rub this herb mixture evenly over the chicken breasts.

2. **Preheat the Smoker**: Preheat your wood pellet smoker grill to 250°F (121°C) using your choice of wood pellets.

3. **Smoke the Chicken Breasts**: Place the seasoned chicken breasts on the smoker grate. Smoke for about 1.5 hours, or until the internal temperature reaches 165°F (74°C).

4. **Rest and Serve**: Remove the chicken breasts from the smoker and let them rest for 5-10 minutes before slicing and serving.

Macronutrients (per serving, approximate):

Calories: 230 kcal - **Carbohydrates**: 1g - **Protein**: 35g - **Fat**: 9g

CHERRY WOOD SMOKED CHICKEN DRUMSTICKS

Preparation Time: 20 minutes (plus optional marinating time)

Cooking Time: 1.5 hours

Servings: 4-6

Ingredients:

- 12 chicken drumsticks
- 1/4 cup olive oil
- For the marinade:
  - 1/4 cup soy sauce
  - 1/4 cup honey
  - 2 tablespoons apple cider vinegar
  - 2 cloves garlic, minced
  - 1 teaspoon smoked paprika
  - 1 teaspoon garlic powder
  - 1 teaspoon onion powder
  - Salt and pepper to taste
- Cherry wood pellets for smoking

Directions:

1. **Prepare the Drumsticks**: In a bowl, whisk together olive oil, soy sauce, honey, apple cider vinegar, minced garlic, smoked paprika, garlic powder, onion powder, salt, and pepper. Coat the chicken drumsticks in the marinade. For more flavor, marinate in the refrigerator for 1-2 hours (optional).

2. **Preheat the Smoker**: Preheat your wood pellet smoker grill to 250°F (121°C) using cherry wood pellets.

3. **Smoke the Drumsticks**: Place the chicken drumsticks on the smoker grate. Smoke for about 1.5 hours, or until the internal temperature reaches 165°F (74°C) and the skin is nicely caramelized.

4. **Rest and Serve**: Remove the drumsticks from the smoker and let them rest for a few minutes before serving.

Macronutrients (per serving, approximate):

Calories: 300 kcal - **Carbohydrates:** 8g - **Protein:** 27g - **Fat:** 18g

SMOKED BBQ CHICKEN LEGS

Preparation Time: 20 minutes

Cooking Time: 2 hours

Servings: 4-6

Ingredients:

- 8 chicken legs
- 1/2 cup BBQ sauce (your choice)
- 2 tablespoons olive oil
- 1 tablespoon brown sugar
- 1 tablespoon paprika
- 1 teaspoon garlic powder
- 1 teaspoon onion powder
- 1/2 teaspoon cayenne pepper (optional, for heat)
- Salt and black pepper to taste
- Your choice of wood pellets for smoking (applewood or hickory work well)

Directions:

1. **Prepare the Chicken**: In a small bowl, mix together brown sugar, paprika, garlic powder, onion powder, cayenne pepper, salt, and black pepper. Rub each chicken leg with olive oil, then coat with the spice mixture.

2. **Preheat the Smoker**: Preheat your wood pellet smoker grill to 250°F (121°C) using your choice of wood pellets.

3. **Smoke the Chicken Legs**: Place the seasoned chicken legs on the smoker grate. Smoke for about 1.5 hours.

4. **Glaze the Chicken**: Brush the chicken legs with BBQ sauce and continue smoking for another 30 minutes, or until the internal temperature reaches 165°F (74°C).

5. **Rest and Serve**: Let the chicken legs rest for a few minutes before serving.

Macronutrients (per serving, approximate):

Calories: 320 kcal - **Carbohydrates**: 12g - **Protein**: 25g - **Fat**: 18g

PECAN WOOD SMOKED CHICKEN QUARTERS

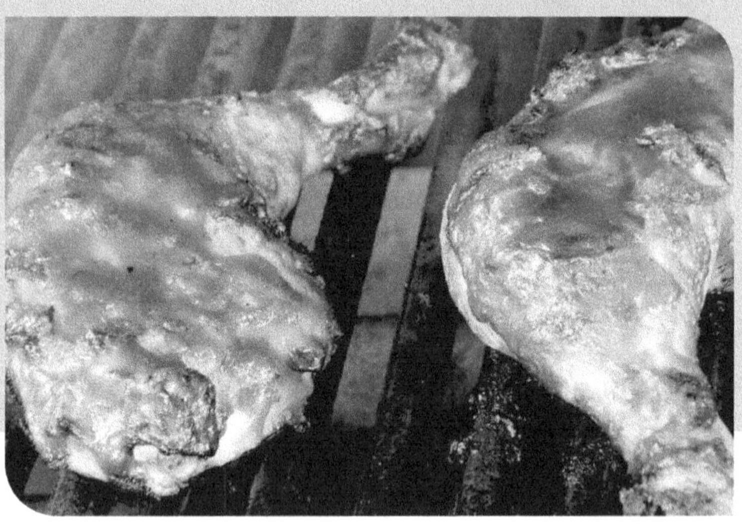

Preparation Time: 20 minutes

Cooking Time: 3 hours

Servings: 4-6

Ingredients:

- 4 chicken leg quarters
- 1/4 cup olive oil
- For the rub:
  - 2 tablespoons brown sugar
  - 1 tablespoon smoked paprika
  - 1 tablespoon garlic powder
  - 1 tablespoon onion powder
  - 1 teaspoon dried thyme
  - 1 teaspoon dried oregano
  - Salt and black pepper to taste
- Pecan wood pellets for smoking

Directions:

1. **Prepare the Chicken**: Pat the chicken quarters dry with paper towels. In a small bowl, mix together the ingredients for the rub. Coat each chicken quarter with olive oil and then apply the rub evenly on all sides.

2. **Preheat the Smoker**: Preheat your wood pellet smoker grill to 250°F (121°C) using pecan wood pellets.

3. **Smoke the Chicken Quarters**: Place the chicken quarters on the smoker grate, skin side up. Smoke for about 3 hours, or until the internal temperature of the chicken reaches 165°F (74°C).

4. **Rest and Serve**: Let the chicken quarters rest for 10 minutes after removing them from the smoker. This allows the juices to redistribute.

Macronutrients (per serving, approximate):

Calories: 400 kcal - **Carbohydrates**: 5g - **Protein**: 35g - **Fat**: 26g

SPICY SMOKED CHICKEN TACOS

Preparation Time: 20 minutes (plus optional marinating time)

Cooking Time: 2 hours

Servings: 4-6

Ingredients:

- 4 boneless, skinless chicken breasts
- For the marinade:
  - 1/4 cup lime juice
  - 2 tablespoons olive oil
  - 2 tablespoons hot sauce or chipotle in adobo sauce
  - 2 cloves garlic, minced
  - 1 teaspoon cumin
  - 1 teaspoon smoked paprika
  - Salt and pepper to taste
- Taco shells or tortillas
- Toppings: shredded lettuce, diced tomatoes, avocado, shredded cheese, sour cream, etc.
- Your choice of wood pellets for smoking (applewood or hickory work well)

Directions:

1. **Marinate the Chicken**: In a bowl, combine lime juice, olive oil, hot sauce, garlic, cumin, smoked paprika, salt, and pepper. Add the chicken breasts, ensuring they are well coated. Marinate for at least 30 minutes, preferably 1-2 hours.

2. **Preheat the Smoker**: Preheat your wood pellet smoker grill to 250°F (121°C) using your choice of wood pellets.

3. **Smoke the Chicken**: Remove the chicken from the marinade and place it on the smoker grate. Smoke for about 2 hours, or until the internal temperature reaches 165°F (74°C).

4. **Assemble the Tacos**: Shred the smoked chicken and serve in taco shells or tortillas with your favorite toppings.

Macronutrients (per serving, approximate, excluding taco shells and toppings):

Calories: 230 kcal - **Carbohydrates**: 3g - **Protein**: 26g - **Fat**: 12g

CHAPTER 6
TURKEY RECIPES

APPLEWOOD SMOKED WHOLE TURKEY

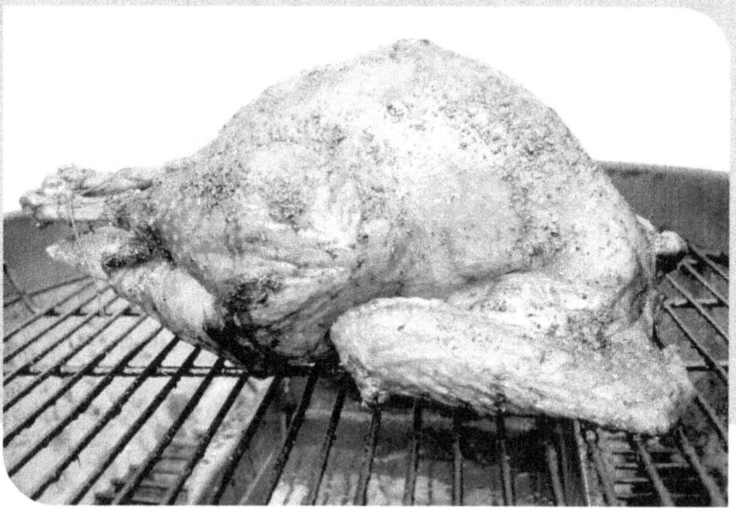

Preparation Time: 1 hour (plus overnight brining)

Cooking Time: 4-5 hours

Servings: 8-10

Ingredients:

- 1 whole turkey (about 12-14 pounds)
- For the brine:
  - 1 gallon water
  - 1 cup kosher salt
  - 1/2 cup brown sugar
  - 1 tablespoon black peppercorns
  - 2 bay leaves
  - 1 onion, quartered
  - 4 cloves garlic, smashed
- For the rub:
  - 2 tablespoons olive oil
  - 1 tablespoon smoked paprika
  - 1 teaspoon garlic powder
  - 1 teaspoon onion powder
  - 1 teaspoon dried thyme
  - Salt and pepper to taste
- Applewood pellets for smoking

Directions:

1. **Brine the Turkey**: Combine all brine ingredients in a large pot and bring to a simmer until salt and sugar are dissolved. Cool completely. Submerge the turkey in the brine and refrigerate overnight.

2. **Preheat the Smoker**: Preheat your wood pellet smoker grill to 250°F (121°C) using applewood pellets.

3. **Prepare the Turkey**: Remove the turkey from the brine, rinse thoroughly, and pat dry. Mix the rub ingredients and coat the turkey evenly inside and out.

4. **Smoke the Turkey**: Place the turkey on the smoker grate. Smoke for about 4-5 hours, or until the internal temperature in the thickest part of the breast reaches 165°F (74°C).

5. **Rest and Serve**: Let the turkey rest for 20-30 minutes before carving.

Macronutrients (per serving, approximate):

Calories: 450 kcal - **Carbohydrates**: 0g - **Protein**: 70g - **Fat**: 20g

HICKORY SMOKED TURKEY BREAST

Preparation Time: 30 minutes

Cooking Time: 3-4 hours

Servings: 6-8

Ingredients:

- 1 bone-in turkey breast (about 5-6 pounds)
- 2 tablespoons olive oil
- 1 tablespoon brown sugar
- 1 tablespoon smoked paprika
- 1 teaspoon garlic powder
- 1 teaspoon onion powder
- 1 teaspoon dried thyme
- Salt and black pepper to taste
- Hickory wood pellets for smoking

Directions:

1. **Prepare the Turkey Breast**: Pat the turkey breast dry with paper towels. In a small bowl, mix together brown sugar, smoked paprika, garlic powder, onion powder, thyme, salt, and black pepper. Rub the turkey breast with olive oil and then apply the seasoning mix evenly over the surface.

2. **Preheat the Smoker**: Preheat your wood pellet smoker grill to 250°F (121°C) using hickory wood pellets.

3. **Smoke the Turkey Breast**: Place the seasoned turkey breast on the smoker grate, skin side up. Smoke for about 3-4 hours, or until the internal temperature of the thickest part of the breast reaches 165°F (74°C).

4. **Rest and Serve**: Remove the turkey breast from the smoker and let it rest for 20 minutes before slicing.

Macronutrients (per serving, approximate):

Calories: 300 kcal - **Carbohydrates:** 2g - **Protein:** 45g - **Fat:** 12g

MESQUITE SMOKED TURKEY LEGS

Preparation Time: 20 minutes (plus optional overnight brining)

Cooking Time: 4 hours

Servings: 4-6

Ingredients:

- 6 turkey legs
- For the optional brine:
  - 1 gallon water
  - 1 cup kosher salt
  - 1/2 cup brown sugar
  - 1 tablespoon black peppercorns
  - 2 bay leaves
- For the rub:
  - 2 tablespoons olive oil
  - 2 tablespoons brown sugar
  - 1 tablespoon smoked paprika
  - 1 teaspoon garlic powder
  - 1 teaspoon onion powder
  - Salt and black pepper to taste
- Mesquite wood pellets for smoking

Directions:

1. **Optional Brine**: If brining, dissolve salt and brown sugar in water, add peppercorns and bay leaves, and bring to a simmer. Cool completely and brine the turkey legs in the mixture overnight in the refrigerator.

2. **Preheat the Smoker**: Preheat your wood pellet smoker grill to 225°F (107°C) using mesquite wood pellets.

3. **Prepare the Turkey Legs**: If brined, rinse the legs and pat dry. Rub each leg with olive oil. Mix brown sugar, smoked paprika, garlic powder, onion powder, salt, and black pepper, and apply this rub evenly on the turkey legs.

4. **Smoke the Turkey Legs**: Place the seasoned turkey legs on the smoker grate. Smoke for about 4 hours, or until the internal temperature reaches 165°F (74°C).

5. **Rest and Serve**: Let the turkey legs rest for a few minutes before serving.

Macronutrients (per serving, approximate):

Calories: 350 kcal - **Carbohydrates**: 5g - **Protein**: 45g - **Fat**: 16g

SMOKED TURKEY AND HERB SAUSAGE

Preparation Time: 45 minutes

Cooking Time: 3 hours

Servings: 6-8

Ingredients:

- 2 pounds ground turkey
- 1/2 pound pork fatback, finely chopped
- 2 cloves garlic, minced
- 2 tablespoons fresh sage, finely chopped
- 2 tablespoons fresh thyme, finely chopped
- 1 tablespoon smoked paprika
- 1 teaspoon fennel seeds, crushed
- 1 teaspoon red pepper flakes (optional for heat)
- Salt and pepper to taste
- Natural sausage casings (optional)
- Your choice of wood pellets for smoking (applewood or hickory work well)

Directions:

1. **Prepare the Sausage Mixture**: In a large bowl, combine ground turkey, pork fatback, minced garlic, sage, thyme, smoked paprika, crushed fennel seeds, red pepper flakes, salt, and pepper. Mix well.

2. **Stuff the Sausages**: If using casings, stuff the sausage mixture into the casings and twist to form individual sausages. If not using casings, form the mixture into sausage shapes.

3. **Preheat the Smoker**: Preheat your wood pellet smoker grill to 225°F (107°C) using your choice of wood pellets.

4. **Smoke the Sausages**: Place the sausages on the smoker grate. Smoke for about 3 hours, or until the internal temperature reaches 165°F (74°C).

5. **Rest and Serve**: Let the sausages rest for a few minutes before serving.

Macronutrients (per serving, approximate):

70

Calories: 300 kcal - **Carbohydrates:** 1g - **Protein:** 25g - **Fat:** 22g

CHERRY WOOD SMOKED TURKEY WINGS

Preparation Time: 20 minutes (plus optional marinating time)

Cooking Time: 2.5 hours

Servings: 4-6

Ingredients:

- 6 turkey wings, split at the joints
- For the marinade:
  - 1/4 cup olive oil
  - 1/4 cup soy sauce
  - 1/4 cup honey
  - 2 tablespoons apple cider vinegar
  - 1 tablespoon garlic powder
  - 1 tablespoon smoked paprika
  - 1 teaspoon dried thyme
  - Salt and pepper to taste
- Cherry wood pellets for smoking

Directions:

1. **Marinate the Turkey Wings**: In a large bowl, whisk together olive oil, soy sauce, honey, apple cider vinegar, garlic powder, smoked paprika, dried thyme, salt, and pepper. Add the turkey wings and toss to coat evenly. Marinate for at least 1 hour, preferably overnight.

2. **Preheat the Smoker**: Preheat your wood pellet smoker grill to 250°F (121°C) using cherry wood pellets.

3. **Smoke the Turkey Wings**: Remove the wings from the marinade and place them on the smoker grate. Smoke for about 2.5 hours, or until the wings are golden brown and the internal temperature reaches 165°F (74°C).

4. **Rest and Serve**: Let the turkey wings rest for a few minutes before serving.

Macronutrients (per serving, approximate):

Calories: 400 kcal - **Carbohydrates**: 10g - **Protein**: 35g - **Fat**: 24g

SMOKED TURKEY MEATLOAF

Preparation Time: 20 minutes

Cooking Time: 3 hours

Servings: 6-8

Ingredients:

- 2 pounds ground turkey
- 1 cup breadcrumbs
- 1/2 cup milk
- 1 onion, finely chopped
- 2 cloves garlic, minced
- 1 egg, beaten
- 1/4 cup ketchup
- 2 tablespoons Worcestershire sauce
- 1 tablespoon Dijon mustard
- 1 teaspoon smoked paprika
- 1 teaspoon dried thyme
- Salt and black pepper to taste
- Your choice of wood pellets for smoking (applewood or hickory work well)

Directions:

1. **Prepare the Meatloaf Mixture**: In a large bowl, combine ground turkey, breadcrumbs, milk, onion, garlic, egg, ketchup, Worcestershire sauce, Dijon mustard, smoked paprika, thyme, salt, and black pepper. Mix until well combined but avoid overmixing.

2. **Shape the Meatloaf**: Form the mixture into a loaf on a sheet of aluminum foil or in a suitable meatloaf pan.

3. **Preheat the Smoker**: Preheat your wood pellet smoker grill to 250°F (121°C) using your choice of wood pellets.

4. **Smoke the Meatloaf**: Place the meatloaf on the smoker grate. Smoke for about 3 hours, or until the internal temperature reaches 165°F (74°C).

5. **Rest and Serve**: Let the meatloaf rest for 10 minutes before slicing and serving.

Macronutrients (per serving, approximate):

Calories: 280 kcal - **Carbohydrates:** 15g - **Protein:** 27g - **Fat:** 12g

SMOKED TURKEY CHILI

Preparation Time: 20 minutes

Cooking Time: 4 hours

Servings: 6-8

Ingredients:

- 2 pounds ground turkey
- 1 large onion, chopped
- 2 cloves garlic, minced
- 2 cans (15 oz each) kidney beans, drained and rinsed
- 1 can (28 oz) crushed tomatoes
- 1 can (15 oz) tomato sauce
- 2 tablespoons chili powder
- 1 tablespoon cumin
- 1 teaspoon smoked paprika
- 1/2 teaspoon cayenne pepper (optional, for heat)
- Salt and black pepper to taste
- 2 cups chicken broth
- Your choice of wood pellets for smoking (hickory or mesquite work well)
- Optional toppings: shredded cheese, sour cream, green onions, cilantro

Directions:

1. **Prepare the Chili Mixture**: In a large bowl, mix together the ground turkey, chopped onion, minced garlic, kidney beans, crushed tomatoes, tomato sauce, chili powder, cumin, smoked paprika, cayenne pepper, salt, and black pepper.

2. **Preheat the Smoker**: Preheat your wood pellet smoker grill to 225°F (107°C) using your choice of wood pellets.

3. **Smoke the Chili**: Transfer the chili mixture to a large cast-iron pot or dutch oven. Stir in the chicken broth. Place the pot on the smoker grate. Smoke for about 4 hours, stirring occasionally.

4. **Finish and Serve**: After 4 hours, check the consistency and flavor of the chili. Adjust seasonings if needed. Serve hot with your choice of toppings.

Macronutrients (per serving, approximate):

Calories: 330 kcal - **Carbohydrates**: 28g - **Protein**: 27g - **Fat**: 12g

SMOKED TURKEY STUFFED PEPPERS

Preparation Time: 25 minutes

Cooking Time: 2 hours

Servings: 4-6

Ingredients:

- 4 large bell peppers, tops cut off and seeds removed
- 1 pound ground turkey
- 1 cup cooked quinoa or rice
- 1 can (15 oz) black beans, drained and rinsed
- 1 cup corn kernels (fresh or frozen)
- 1/2 cup salsa
- 1 teaspoon cumin
- 1 teaspoon smoked paprika
- Salt and pepper to taste
- 1 cup shredded cheddar cheese
- Your choice of wood pellets for smoking (applewood or cherry work well)

Directions:

1. **Prepare the Filling**: In a large bowl, mix together the ground turkey, cooked quinoa or rice, black beans, corn, salsa, cumin, smoked paprika, salt, and pepper.

2. **Stuff the Peppers**: Spoon the filling into each bell pepper. Top each pepper with shredded cheddar cheese.

3. **Preheat the Smoker**: Preheat your wood pellet smoker grill to 250°F (121°C) using your choice of wood pellets.

4. **Smoke the Stuffed Peppers**: Place the stuffed peppers on the smoker grate. Smoke for about 2 hours, or until the peppers are tender and the filling is cooked through.

5. **Serve**: Serve the smoked stuffed peppers hot, with additional salsa or sour cream if desired.

Macronutrients (per serving, approximate):

Calories: 350 kcal - **Carbohydrates**: 35g - **Protein**: 25g - **Fat**: 15g

CHAPTER 7
SEAFOOD RECIPES

HICKORY SMOKED SALMON FILLETS

Preparation Time: 15 minutes (plus optional brining time)

Cooking Time: 1 hour

Servings: 4

Ingredients:

- 4 salmon fillets (about 6 ounces each)
- 2 tablespoons brown sugar
- 2 tablespoons soy sauce
- 2 tablespoons olive oil
- 1 tablespoon lemon juice
- 1 teaspoon garlic powder
- 1 teaspoon onion powder
- Salt and black pepper to taste
- Hickory wood pellets for smoking

Directions:

1. **Prepare the Salmon**: In a small bowl, whisk together brown sugar, soy sauce, olive oil, lemon juice, garlic powder, onion powder, salt, and black pepper. Brush this mixture over the salmon fillets. For a more intense flavor, let the salmon marinate in the refrigerator for 1-2 hours.

2. **Preheat the Smoker**: Preheat your wood pellet smoker grill to 225°F (107°C) using hickory wood pellets.

3. **Smoke the Salmon**: Place the salmon fillets on the smoker grate, skin side down. Smoke for about 1 hour, or until the internal temperature reaches 145°F (63°C) and the fish flakes easily with a fork.

4. **Rest and Serve**: Remove the salmon from the smoker and let it rest for a few minutes before serving.

Macronutrients (per serving, approximate):

Calories: 300 kcal - **Carbohydrates**: 5g - **Protein**: 23g - **Fat**: 20g

APPLEWOOD SMOKED TROUT

Preparation Time: 15 minutes (plus optional brining time)

Cooking Time: 1.5 to 2 hours

Servings: 4

Ingredients:

- 4 whole trout, cleaned and gutted
- For the optional brine:
  - 4 cups water
  - 1/4 cup kosher salt
  - 1/4 cup sugar
  - 1 lemon, sliced
  - A few sprigs of fresh dill
- For the rub:
  - 2 tablespoons olive oil
  - 1 teaspoon garlic powder
  - 1 teaspoon onion powder
  - Salt and black pepper to taste
- Applewood pellets for smoking

Directions:

1. **Optional Brine**: If brining, dissolve salt and sugar in water, add lemon slices and dill, and bring to a simmer. Cool completely and submerge the trout in the brine for 2-4 hours in the refrigerator.

2. **Preheat the Smoker**: Preheat your wood pellet smoker grill to 225°F (107°C) using applewood pellets.

3. **Prepare the Trout**: If brined, rinse the trout and pat dry. Rub each trout with olive oil and season inside and out with garlic powder, onion powder, salt, and black pepper.

4. **Smoke the Trout**: Place the trout on the smoker grate. Smoke for 1.5 to 2 hours, or until the flesh is opaque and flakes easily.

5. **Rest and Serve**: Remove the trout from the smoker and let it rest for a few minutes before serving.

Macronutrients (per serving, approximate):

Calories: 250 kcal - **Carbohydrates**: 0g - **Protein**: 40g - **Fat**: 8g

CEDAR PLANK SMOKED HALIBUT

Preparation Time: 30 minutes (plus soaking time for the plank)

Cooking Time: 1 hour

Servings: 4

Ingredients:

- 4 halibut fillets (about 6 ounces each)
- 1 cedar plank, suitable for grilling
- 2 tablespoons olive oil
- 1 tablespoon lemon juice
- 1 teaspoon garlic powder
- 1 teaspoon dried dill
- Salt and black pepper to taste
- Lemon slices for garnish
- Your choice of wood pellets for smoking (applewood or cherry work well)

Directions:

1. **Prepare the Cedar Plank**: Soak the cedar plank in water for at least 1 hour before cooking to prevent it from burning.

2. **Preheat the Smoker**: Preheat your wood pellet smoker grill to 225°F (107°C) using your choice of wood pellets.

3. **Season the Halibut**: Brush the halibut fillets with olive oil and lemon juice. Season them with garlic powder, dried dill, salt, and black pepper.

4. **Smoke the Halibut**: Place the soaked cedar plank on the smoker grate and then lay the seasoned halibut fillets on top of the plank. Close the lid and smoke for about 1 hour, or until the halibut is cooked through and flakes easily.

5. **Serve**: Garnish the smoked halibut with lemon slices and serve immediately.

Macronutrients (per serving, approximate):

Calories: 230 kcal - **Carbohydrates**: 1g - **Protein**: 35g - **Fat**: 10g

MESQUITE SMOKED TUNA STEAKS

Preparation Time: 20 minutes

Cooking Time: 45 minutes to 1 hour

Servings: 4

Ingredients:

- 4 tuna steaks (about 6 ounces each)
- 2 tablespoons olive oil
- 2 tablespoons soy sauce
- 1 tablespoon lemon juice
- 2 cloves garlic, minced
- 1 teaspoon ginger, grated
- 1 teaspoon honey
- Salt and black pepper to taste
- Mesquite wood pellets for smoking

Directions:

1. **Marinate the Tuna**: In a bowl, whisk together olive oil, soy sauce, lemon juice, minced garlic, grated ginger, honey, salt, and black pepper. Place the tuna steaks in the marinade, ensuring they are well coated. Let them marinate for at least 15 minutes.

2. **Preheat the Smoker**: Preheat your wood pellet smoker grill to 225°F (107°C) using mesquite wood pellets.

3. **Smoke the Tuna Steaks**: Remove the tuna steaks from the marinade and place them on the smoker grate. Smoke for about 45 minutes to 1 hour, or until the tuna reaches your desired level of doneness.

4. **Rest and Serve**: Let the tuna steaks rest for a few minutes after removing them from the smoker, then serve immediately.

Macronutrients (per serving, approximate):

Calories: 250 kcal - **Carbohydrates**: 3g - **Protein**: 40g - **Fat**: 9g

SMOKED MAHI-MAHI WITH CITRUS GLAZE

Preparation Time: 20 minutes

Cooking Time: 1 to 1.5 hours

Servings: 4

Ingredients:

- 4 mahi-mahi fillets (about 6 ounces each)
- 2 tablespoons olive oil
- For the citrus glaze:
  - 1/4 cup orange juice
  - 1/4 cup lemon juice
  - 2 tablespoons lime juice
  - 2 tablespoons honey
  - 1 teaspoon garlic, minced
  - Salt and pepper to taste
- Your choice of wood pellets for smoking (applewood or cherry work well)

Directions:

1. **Prepare the Citrus Glaze**: In a small saucepan, combine orange juice, lemon juice, lime juice, honey, and minced garlic. Simmer over medium heat until the mixture reduces slightly and thickens into a glaze. Season with salt and pepper.

2. **Preheat the Smoker**: Preheat your wood pellet smoker grill to 225°F (107°C) using your choice of wood pellets.

3. **Season the Mahi-Mahi**: Brush the mahi-mahi fillets with olive oil and season with salt and pepper.

4. **Smoke the Mahi-Mahi**: Place the mahi-mahi fillets on the smoker grate. Smoke for about 1 to 1.5 hours, or until the fish is opaque and flakes easily with a fork.

5. **Glaze and Serve**: In the last 10-15 minutes of smoking, brush the mahi-mahi fillets with the citrus glaze. Serve with additional glaze on the side.

Macronutrients (per serving, approximate):

Calories: 250 kcal - **Carbohydrates**: 10g - **Protein**: 35g - **Fat**: 8g

CHERRY WOOD SMOKED CATFISH

Preparation Time: 20 minutes

Cooking Time: 1.5 to 2 hours

Servings: 4

Ingredients:

- 4 catfish fillets (about 6 ounces each)
- 2 tablespoons olive oil
- 1 tablespoon paprika
- 1 teaspoon garlic powder
- 1 teaspoon onion powder
- 1/2 teaspoon cayenne pepper (optional for heat)
- Salt and black pepper to taste
- Cherry wood pellets for smoking

Directions:

1. **Prepare the Catfish**: Pat the catfish fillets dry with paper towels. In a small bowl, mix together paprika, garlic powder, onion powder, cayenne pepper, salt, and black pepper. Rub each fillet with olive oil, then coat with the spice mixture.

2. **Preheat the Smoker**: Preheat your wood pellet smoker grill to 225°F (107°C) using cherry wood pellets.

3. **Smoke the Catfish**: Place the seasoned catfish fillets on the smoker grate. Smoke for about 1.5 to 2 hours, or until the fish is cooked through and flakes easily with a fork.

4. **Rest and Serve**: Remove the catfish from the smoker and let it rest for a few minutes before serving.

Macronutrients (per serving, approximate):

Calories: 250 kcal - **Carbohydrates:** 1g - **Protein:** 25g - **Fat:** 15g

SMOKED SWORD-FISH WITH HERB BUTTER

Preparation Time: 15 minutes

Cooking Time: 1 hour

Servings: 4

Ingredients:

- 4 swordfish steaks (about 6 ounces each)
- 2 tablespoons olive oil
- Salt and black pepper to taste
- For the herb butter:
  - 4 tablespoons unsalted butter, softened
  - 1 tablespoon fresh parsley, chopped
  - 1 teaspoon fresh thyme, chopped
  - 1 clove garlic, minced
  - Zest of 1 lemon
- Your choice of wood pellets for smoking (applewood or hickory work well)

Directions:

1. **Prepare the Herb Butter:** In a small bowl, mix together the softened butter, chopped parsley, thyme, minced garlic, and lemon zest. Set aside.

2. **Season the Swordfish:** Brush the swordfish steaks with olive oil and season with salt and black pepper.

3. **Preheat the Smoker:** Preheat your wood pellet smoker grill to 225°F (107°C) using your choice of wood pellets.

4. **Smoke the Swordfish:** Place the swordfish steaks on the smoker grate. Smoke for about 1 hour, or until the fish is cooked through and reaches an internal temperature of 145°F (63°C).

5. **Serve with Herb Butter:** Remove the swordfish from the smoker and top each steak with a dollop of the prepared herb butter before serving.

Macronutrients (per serving, approximate):

Calories: 350 kcal - **Carbohydrates:** 1g - **Protein:** 35g - **Fat:** 22g

PECAN WOOD SMOKED SARDINES

Preparation Time: 15 minutes

Cooking Time: 30 minutes to 1 hour

Servings: 4

Ingredients:

- 1 pound fresh sardines, cleaned and gutted
- 2 tablespoons olive oil
- 1 lemon, sliced
- 2 cloves garlic, minced
- 1 teaspoon dried oregano
- Salt and black pepper to taste
- Pecan wood pellets for smoking

Directions:

1. **Prepare the Sardines**: Rinse the sardines and pat them dry. In a small bowl, mix together olive oil, minced garlic, oregano, salt, and black pepper. Brush this mixture over the sardines and inside their cavities. Place a lemon slice inside each sardine.

2. **Preheat the Smoker**: Preheat your wood pellet smoker grill to 225°F (107°C) using pecan wood pellets.

3. **Smoke the Sardines**: Place the seasoned sardines on the smoker grate. Smoke for about 30 minutes to 1 hour, or until the sardines are cooked through and the skin is slightly crispy.

4. **Serve**: Serve the smoked sardines hot, garnished with additional lemon slices if desired.

Macronutrients (per serving, approximate):

Calories: 200 kcal - **Carbohydrates**: 1g - **Protein**: 25g - **Fat**: 11g

SMOKED SEA BASS WITH LEMON PEPPER

Preparation Time: 15 minutes

Cooking Time: 1 hour

Servings: 4

Ingredients:

- 4 sea bass fillets (about 6 ounces each)
- 2 tablespoons olive oil
- 2 tablespoons lemon juice
- 1 tablespoon freshly ground black pepper
- 1 teaspoon garlic powder
- 1 teaspoon onion powder
- Salt to taste
- Lemon slices for garnish
- Your choice of wood pellets for smoking (applewood or cherry work well)

Directions:

1. **Prepare the Sea Bass**: Pat the sea bass fillets dry with paper towels. In a small bowl, mix together olive oil, lemon juice, black pepper, garlic powder, onion powder, and salt. Brush this mixture over both sides of the sea bass fillets.

2. **Preheat the Smoker**: Preheat your wood pellet smoker grill to 225°F (107°C) using your choice of wood pellets.

3. **Smoke the Sea Bass**: Place the seasoned sea bass fillets on the smoker grate. Smoke for about 1 hour, or until the fish is cooked through and flakes easily with a fork.

4. **Serve**: Garnish the smoked sea bass with lemon slices and serve immediately.

Macronutrients (per serving, approximate):

Calories: 230 kcal - **Carbohydrates:** 1g - **Protein:** 35g - **Fat:** 9g

CHAPTER 8
VEGETABLES RECIPES

SMOKED GARLIC PARMESAN ASPARAGUS

Preparation Time: 10 minutes

Cooking Time: 30 minutes

Servings: 4

Ingredients:

- 1 pound fresh asparagus, trimmed
- 2 tablespoons olive oil
- 3 cloves garlic, minced
- 1/4 cup grated Parmesan cheese
- Salt and black pepper to taste
- Your choice of wood pellets for smoking (hickory or applewood work well)

Directions:

1. **Prepare the Asparagus**: In a large bowl, toss the asparagus with olive oil, minced garlic, salt, and black pepper.

2. **Preheat the Smoker**: Preheat your wood pellet smoker grill to 225°F (107°C) using your choice of wood pellets.

3. **Smoke the Asparagus**: Spread the asparagus in a single layer on the smoker grate. Smoke for about 30 minutes, or until the asparagus is tender and slightly charred.

4. **Add Parmesan and Serve**: Once the asparagus is done, sprinkle grated Parmesan cheese over the top while it's still hot. Serve immediately.

Macronutrients (per serving, approximate):

Calories: 100 kcal - **Carbohydrates**: 4g - **Protein**: 4g - **Fat**: 8g

HICKORY SMOKED MAC AND CHEESE

Preparation Time: 20 minutes

Cooking Time: 1 hour

Servings: 6

Ingredients:

- 16 oz elbow macaroni, cooked and drained
- 3 cups cheddar cheese, shredded
- 1 cup Gruyère cheese, shredded
- 2 cups whole milk
- 1/2 cup heavy cream
- 1/4 cup unsalted butter
- 3 tablespoons all-purpose flour
- 1 teaspoon mustard powder
- 1/2 teaspoon smoked paprika
- Salt and black pepper to taste
- Hickory wood pellets for smoking

Directions:

1. **Prepare the Cheese Sauce**: In a saucepan, melt the butter over medium heat. Stir in the flour and cook for 1-2 minutes. Gradually whisk in the milk and cream, and cook until the mixture thickens. Add the mustard powder, smoked paprika, salt, and pepper. Remove from heat and stir in 2 cups of cheddar cheese and all of the Gruyère until melted.

2. **Combine Macaroni and Cheese Sauce**: Mix the cooked macaroni with the cheese sauce, ensuring the pasta is well coated.

3. **Preheat the Smoker**: Preheat your wood pellet smoker grill to 225°F (107°C) using hickory wood pellets.

4. **Smoke the Mac and Cheese**: Transfer the macaroni and cheese mixture to a greased baking dish. Sprinkle the remaining cheddar cheese on top. Place the dish in the smoker and smoke for about 1 hour, or until the top is golden brown and bubbly.

5. **Serve**: Let the mac and cheese cool slightly before serving.

Macronutrients (per serving, approximate):

Calories: 650 kcal - **Carbohydrates**: 50g - **Protein**: 25g - **Fat**: 40g

APPLEWOOD SMOKED SWEET POTATOES

Preparation Time: 15 minutes

Cooking Time: 1.5 to 2 hours

Servings: 4-6

Ingredients:

- 4 large sweet potatoes, washed and dried
- 2 tablespoons olive oil
- 2 tablespoons maple syrup
- 1 teaspoon cinnamon
- 1/2 teaspoon nutmeg
- Salt to taste
- Applewood pellets for smoking

Directions:

1. **Prepare the Sweet Potatoes**: Slice the sweet potatoes into 1/2-inch thick rounds. In a large bowl, toss them with olive oil, maple syrup, cinnamon, nutmeg, and salt.

2. **Preheat the Smoker**: Preheat your wood pellet smoker grill to 225°F (107°C) using applewood pellets.

3. **Smoke the Sweet Potatoes**: Arrange the sweet potato slices in a single layer on the smoker grate. Smoke for about 1.5 to 2 hours, or until they are tender and slightly caramelized.

4. **Serve**: Remove the sweet potatoes from the smoker and serve warm as a delicious side dish.

Macronutrients (per serving, approximate):

Calories: 200 kcal - **Carbohydrates**: 35g - **Protein**: 2g - **Fat**: 5g

MESQUITE SMOKED CORN ON THE COB

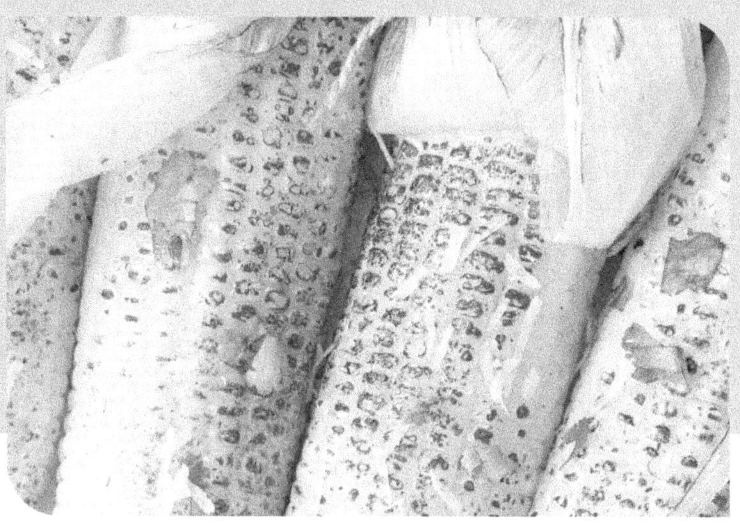

Preparation Time: **10 minutes**

Cooking Time: **1 hour**

Servings: **4**

Ingredients:

- 4 ears of corn, husks and silk removed
- 4 tablespoons butter, softened
- 1 teaspoon smoked paprika
- 1/2 teaspoon garlic powder
- Salt and black pepper to taste
- Mesquite wood pellets for smoking

Directions:

1. **Prepare the Corn**: Rinse the corn and pat dry. In a small bowl, mix together the softened butter, smoked paprika, garlic powder, salt, and black pepper.

2. **Preheat the Smoker**: Preheat your wood pellet smoker grill to 225°F (107°C) using mesquite wood pellets.

3. **Smoke the Corn**: Spread the seasoned butter mixture over each ear of corn. Wrap each ear in aluminum foil. Place the wrapped corn on the smoker grate and smoke for about 1 hour.

4. **Serve**: Carefully unwrap the corn and serve hot as a flavorful and smoky side dish.

Macronutrients (per serving, approximate):

Calories: 200 kcal - **Carbohydrates**: 17g - **Protein**: 3g - **Fat**: 14g

CHERRY WOOD SMOKED BRUSSELS SPROUTS

Preparation Time: 15 minutes

Cooking Time: 1 hour

Servings: 4

Ingredients:

- 1 pound Brussels sprouts, trimmed and halved
- 2 tablespoons olive oil
- 2 tablespoons balsamic vinegar
- 1 tablespoon honey
- 1 teaspoon garlic powder
- Salt and black pepper to taste
- Cherry wood pellets for smoking

Directions:

1. **Prepare the Brussels Sprouts**: In a large bowl, toss the Brussels sprouts with olive oil, balsamic vinegar, honey, garlic powder, salt, and black pepper until well coated.

2. **Preheat the Smoker**: Preheat your wood pellet smoker grill to 225°F (107°C) using cherry wood pellets.

3. **Smoke the Brussels Sprouts**: Spread the Brussels sprouts in a single layer on a grill mat or aluminum foil placed on the smoker grate. Smoke for about 1 hour, or until they are tender and caramelized.

4. **Serve**: Remove the Brussels sprouts from the smoker and serve as a delicious and flavorful side dish.

Macronutrients (per serving, approximate):

Calories: 120 kcal - **Carbohydrates**: 14g - **Protein**: 3g - **Fat**: 7g

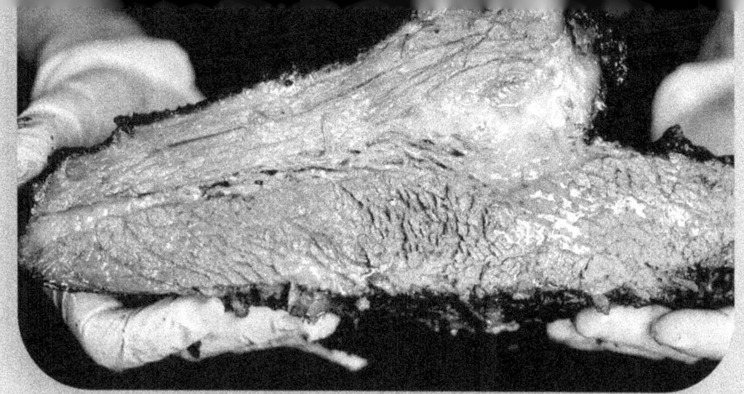

Conclusion

Congratulations on completing the entire cookbook! You now possess every secret to mastering the art of cooking with a Wood Pellet Smoker-Grill. Armed with a plethora of fantastic recipes, you're set to embark on a culinary journey, revisiting these dishes time and time again. The beauty of this smoker-grill is its consistency in delivering delicious flavors every time, as long as you precisely follow the listed ingredients and instructions.

To maximize the potential of your Wood Pellet Smoker-Grill, start by familiarizing yourself with its operation and understanding its benefits. This knowledge will empower you to fully leverage the equipment in your cooking endeavors. The cookbook offers a diverse range of recipes, including poultry, red meat, pork, and seafood, allowing you to experiment with different dishes daily and hone your cooking skills. Diverse cooking methods like smoking, grilling, and searing are covered, with straightforward instructions for each recipe.

Proper storage of your wood pellets is crucial. Keep them in a dry place, such as a shed or garage, to prevent moisture from compromising their quality. Moisture can lead to the pellets getting wet and degrading, which not only affects their ability to ignite but can also damage your smoker's auger.

Remember, for optimal results, it's advisable to use foil on your grease drip pan. Replace the foil after two to four cooking sessions or after a long cooking session. If you choose not to use foil, ensure to regularly clean any residue buildup on the drip pan to avoid burning off old, rancid grease, which can negatively affect your food's flavor.

When it comes to pork, sweet flavors are a fantastic match. I often recommend using local honey, which supports beekeepers and farmers while providing superior taste. Brown sugar and Canadian maple syrup, which I like to pick up on trips to Toronto, also pair beautifully with pork dishes.

In barbecue, the type of fuel is key to flavor. While smokers typically use wood, charcoal, or pellets, electric or gas smoker grills are also popular. Hardwoods like hickory or oak are ideal for achieving the best flavor.

Now, it's time to choose your first recipe from this cookbook. Whether you're a fan of seafood or red meat, or you're eager to try every recipe, the journey promises to be exciting and delicious. So, what will your first choice be?

SCAN
the QR code Below
to download your
2 FREE bonus

No email is required

Thank you for your purchase.
If you enjoyed my book, I would be grateful
if you could *leave an honest review on Amazon*